THE AWARD OF WILLIAM ALNWICK,

BISHOP OF LINCOLN, A.D. 1439

THE AWARD OF WILLIAM ALNWICK,

BISHOP OF LINCOLN, A.D. 1439

EDITED AND TRANSLATED

by

REGINALD MAXWELL WOOLLEY, B.D.
Rector and Vicar of Minting

WITH A PREFACE, INTRODUCTION AND CHRONOLOGICAL TABLE

by

CHRISTOPHER WORDSWORTH, M.A.
Subdean of Sarum and Master of St Nicholas' Hospital, Salisbury

Cambridge
at the University Press
1913

CAMBRIDGE
UNIVERSITY PRESS

University Printing House, Cambridge CB2 8BS, United Kingdom

Cambridge University Press is part of the University of Cambridge.

It furthers the University's mission by disseminating knowledge in the pursuit of education, learning and research at the highest international levels of excellence.

www.cambridge.org
Information on this title: www.cambridge.org/9781107448179

© Cambridge University Press 1913

This publication is in copyright. Subject to statutory exception and to the provisions of relevant collective licensing agreements, no reproduction of any part may take place without the written permission of Cambridge University Press.

First published 1913
First paperback edition 2014

A catalogue record for this publication is available from the British Library

ISBN 978-1-107-44817-9 Paperback

Cambridge University Press has no responsibility for the persistence or accuracy of URLs for external or third-party internet websites referred to in this publication, and does not guarantee that any content on such websites is, or will remain, accurate or appropriate.

PREFACE

THE Latin Text of Bishop Alnwick's Award, or *Laudum*, has been already issued twice—in the first instance by my Father, Dr Christopher Wordsworth (Bishop of Lincoln, 1869–85) in *Statuta Ecclesiae Cathedralis Lincolniensis* (8vo, Londini, 1873, pp. xvi+112), which contains the 'Novum Registrum' and the 'Laudum Willelmi Alnwick' (as well as the 'Statuta Vicariorum' and five little documents of the 14th and 15th centuries). On the second occasion the Award was edited by myself, in continuation of the work begun by Henry Bradshaw, in volume III. of *Lincoln Cathedral Statutes* (Cambridge, 1892–7).

The present Edition, giving for the first time an English translation, was undertaken at the request of the Dean and Chapter of Lincoln, who considered that after the lapse of forty years there was again need for a convenient edition of this Award which all who are collated to stalls in the Cathedral church are called upon at the time of their installation to promise to obey.

They have been fortunate in securing the services of a Lincolnshire Rector, possessing such literary experience as Mr Woolley has acquired, to make an intelligible English version from the cramped and involved sentences of the notary's Latin text, some of the constructions certified by Thomas Colston being sufficient to make the heart of the stoutest translator quail. Such difficulties in the Latin may be in part attributable to some want of scholarship in the scribe himself, but I am inclined to suppose that the

Bishop's Registrar transcribed faithfully the documents which had been handed to him and certified by Robert Stretton the Chapter-clerk and Thomas Atkyn the Dean's notary on behalf of the two parties then contending and eagerly awaiting a decision from the Bishop. But even in the first part of the troublous reign of King Henry the Sixth the Dean and the Canons at Lincoln had already banded themselves in contrary parts, too ready 'to begin their ancient bickerings'; and often for some 'slight and frivolous cause' those 'factious emulations would arise' which, among other results, render the combatants incapable of weighing well their words. And, in a stormy atmosphere so highly charged, a Bishop called in, as Alnwick was, to arbitrate, might be excused if once and again he uttered and let pass a sentence which calmer revision would condemn, but which might pass muster while he was intent upon understanding the local circumstances and the points at issue between those who recognised his spiritual fatherhood, and while he was doubtlessly filled with such an aspiration as Shakespeare's Duke of Exeter expresses,

"And I, I hope, shall reconcile them all."

Our thanks are due to the Cambridge University Press as well for the care and skill employed in producing the book now presented to the reader, as also for the free scope allowed us in reproducing those portions of the volumes of *Lincoln Cathedral Statutes* which relate to the Lincoln Awards and to the *Laudum* of Bishop Alnwick in particular, with the facsimile of Colston's mark.

Mr Woolley suggests that it may be added that readers who may be sufficiently interested by the perusal of the introduction and the award here printed, and who desire further knowledge of the history of the times when the award was made, and of the general conditions of the

Cathedral and its Chapter, may be referred to the three volumes of *Lincoln Cathedral Statutes* mentioned above: likewise, to the volumes of *Calendars of Papal Registers*, a series still in progress, to the editors whereof, and especially to Mr J. A. Twemlow, as also to the Very Reverend Joseph Armitage Robinson, D.D. (Dean of Wells), we have elsewhere acknowledged our obligation.

He would wish also to join me in thanking the Dean and other members of the Chapter of the 'City set on an Hill,' who have enabled us to work together in the present congenial task.

CHR. WORDSWORTH.

SALISBURY,
St Luke's Day, 1913.

THE DECLARATION MADE IN LINCOLN CATHEDRAL CHURCH ON THE OCCASION OF AN INSTALLATION.

"I, *A. B.* Canon of this Cathedral Church of the Blessed Virgin Mary of Lincoln, and Prebendary of the Prebend of *N.* founded therein,—

(*Or* 'I, *A. B.* Archdeacon of the Archdeaconry of *C.* founded in this Cathedral Church of the Blessed Virgin Mary of Lincoln':—

Or 'I, *A. B.* appointed to the Dignity of *D.* and Canon of this Church':—)

"do solemnly declare that I will be faithful to this Church and Chapter, and obedient to the Dean, as Dean, and to his successors, and in his absence or neglect, to the Chapter of this Church; that I will [to the best of my power][1] observe all the Ordinances[2] and reasonable and approved Customs[3] of the same; [4]that I will faithfully perform the duties of my said Prebend, especially by preaching in this Church at the time appointed to the holder of it[5]. Furthermore[6] I will to my best assist in defending the rights of this Church; and, so[7] far as in me lies and

[1] These words occur in the *Form for Installing a Dignitary* (*whether* Precentor, Chancellor, *or* Sub-dean) as printed by Mr Williamson, Lincoln, in 1895, and likewise in the *Form for Installing as* Archdeacon a person already a Canon. The Declaration of the Dean at his Installation, 1910, printed by W. K. Morton and Sons, Lincoln, is similar to that of the other Dignitaries (only of course omitting the clause of obedience to the Dean).

[2] 'all the Statutes, Ordinances': *Installation of an Archdeacon.*

[3] 'ancient approved and reasonable Customs and Privileges': *Installation of Dignitaries* (1895), and of *the Dean of Lincoln* (1910).

[4–6] A Dignitary here promises to keep Residence, to contribute to the defence of the Rights of the Church, as well as to cause the Ordinances &c. to be observed by others.

[5] The *Statutum de Concionatoribus*, a copy whereof is given to each Canon at his Installation, may be found in *Lincoln Cathedral Statutes*, Camb. 1897, iii. 630–636; or in the *Lincoln Diocesan Kalendar.*

[7] 'and that, as far': *Installation of an Archdeacon.* 'and, as far... lawfully may, that': 1895.

I lawfully may, I will inviolably observe the **Laudum** or Award of the Venerable Father in God [of pious memory][1], William Alnwick, sometime Bishop of Lincoln, and all the contents thereof; nor will I[2] give my assistance, advice, or encouragement to any person or persons whatsoever, desiring or endeavouring to violate that **Laudum**, or [to] contravene the same."

After the act of Installing:—

" *Then, all standing up, the Person Installed also rising, the Person Installing shall turn him, and say*:—

Look upon the titles of the Psalms, which you are to recite every day[3] if nothing hinders."

[1] 'of pious memory': These words are in the forms of 1895, 1910.

[2] 'and that I will not': 1895, 1910.

[3] The list which shows how the Psalms are apportioned among the Prebendaries of Lincoln for a daily recitation of the Psalter with the Litany, is printed in the *Lincoln Diocesan Kalendar*. The form of prayer prescribed by St Hugh to be said by each Canon after his Psalm or Psalms will be found, together with its translation (by Archbishop Benson, formerly prebendary of Heydour and Chancellor), printed on pp. 172, 173, at the end of this present book.

We are indebted to M. H. Footman, Esq., the Chapter Clerk, for a copy of the Forms of Installation.

CONTENTS

ERRATA, &c.

p. 32 n. 4. It appears from Dr J. C. Cox's *Catalogue of Muniments of the D. and C. of Lichfield* (Hist. Collections of Stafford, W. Salt Archæol. Soc. Part ii. vol. vi., 1886, p. 91), that '*le Black Book*' is, at Lichfield, the name of their 3rd vol. of Chapter Acts, 1490—1523; but as it extends only to 131+12 folios, it seems doubtful whether it is the book to which Mr Reynolds was referring. Dr Cox notes the occurrence at f. 288^{b} of the Lichfield *magnum Registrum Album* (a MS. *cir.* 1327) of a note of "Customs of different Cathedral Churches as to guarding the temporalities and spiritualities during vacancies of the see: Wells, Hereford, London, Lincoln, Salisbury, Exeter."

pp. 57-71, *for* because *introducing the several complaints of the Canons against the Dean*, *read* that.

p. 71 ll. 21, 22, *for* to the damage of the same while your visitation was impending, *read* pending your visitation, to the prejudice thereof.

p. 73 ll. 19, 20, *for* through [the growth of] some contrarient [yet] reasonable and legitimate use, *read* through reasonable and legitimate usage to the contrary.

p. 73 l. 28, *after* arbitrator *read* awarder, definer, etc.

p. 75 l. 23 *for* pecuniary, penalty *read* pecuniary, censure.

p. 75 last line *for* even under, *read* and to.

p. 77 l. 11 *for* judgement, *read* custom.

p. 77 l. 18 *for* With regard to these, *read* Furthermore.

p. 79 l. 1 *for* our, *read* a.

p. 80 l. 10 *for* faciendi *read* faciendum.

p. 97 l. 23 *for* all the foregoing *read* all [thereof], as foregoing.

p. 103 l. 4 *for* because *read* that.

p. 129 ll. 26, 27, *omit* from fellowship with the Chapter or.

INTRODUCTION

The Lauda or Awards.

For some time in the twelfth and thirteenth centuries the Bishops of Lincoln were almost invariably appointed from among the Canons. Thus we find R. de Chesney, Geoffrey (elect), and Walter de Coutances, archdeacons; (St Hugh, a Cistercian prior), W. of Blois, precentor; (Hugh de Welles[1]), R. Grosseteste, archd.; H. de Lexington, R. de Gravesend, and Oliver Sutton, deans; J. de Dalderby, chancellor; (Ant. Beek, dean, elected Bishop, was compelled by the Pope's influence to make way for H. Burghersh, a canon of York); T. Beek, canon; J. Gynwell, and J. de Bokyngham, archdeacons.

At the end of the fourteenth century a change was made in the appointments, and from 1398 onward (with some exceptions)[2] a stranger has usually been elected. Though such infusion of new blood must oftentimes have been salutary for the body corporate,—as notably it was when St Hugh, the prior of Witham, was introduced from Somersetshire,—it did not always tell in favour of the peace and harmony of the Chapter, when one *non de gremio Lincolniensis ecclesiae* had been designated as the Bishop.

Litigation between Bishop and Chapter was sharp, no doubt, in the time of Robert Grosseteste, who, before his

[1] According to J. de Schalby's brief memoir, Hugh de Welles had been 'Regis Anglie Cancellarius.' Dimock (*Girald. Cambr.* vii. p. 203) proposes to read 'Clericus.'

[2] So far as Le Neve's *Fasti* informs us, there have been as many as eight *gremial* Bishops of Lincoln between 1452 and the present day. The latest instance was in 1761 when a dean of Lincoln was made Bishop of this Church.

election to the see, had been prebendary and archdeacon for fourteen or fifteen years at Lincoln (as well as at Salisbury), but the points in controversy were set at rest at the expense of an appeal to Rome, accompanied, it is said, by the single unworthy action in that brave man's public career, the payment of bribes to procure the course of justice. The result has been, that each successive Bishop of Lincoln has had secured to him a position, not only as Visitor, but as, in all respects, the *principale caput* of the Chapter; and his preeminence at Lincoln has been long since established more firmly than that of the Bishop in some of the sister Churches, where the Bishop is in certain respects dependent on the Chapter even after his election.

The *Chapter-House* at Lincoln, in the opinion of the late Precentor Venables, was begun in the time of Bp Hugh de Welles, about the year 1225, and finished in Grosseteste's time, 1250. A *parvum capitulum* (not improbably of earlier date than the great Chapter-House) was in existence in 1271, when 'mats for the little chapter [house]' enter into the accounts of Jordan de Ingham. Let us take note now of some of the Visitations and other meetings which may, in all probability, have been held therein in former days.

Apart from Royal and Metropolitical Visitations, the Dean and Chapter of Lincoln had been visited in

1246 by Bp R. Grosseteste.

Cir. 1280—90 by Oliver Sutton, twice. See *Linc. Cath. Stat.* II. pp. lxxix, lxxxv.

Cir. 1292—1304, 1307, 1316, and at some intermediate date, by J. de Dalderby.

[1301. Feb. 25, the Parliament of K. Edward I. met at Lincoln in the Chapter-House.]

[1310. March—June. The Trial of the Knights Templars was conducted in the Chapter-House.]

[1316. Parliament of K. Edw. II. in the Chapter-House.]

1331. Bp Burghersh's General Meeting, attended by Dean and 14 Canons (besides 15 by proxy). A. 2. 23, lf. 18^b.

1334. H. Burghersh.

1437. W. Alnwick. (See *L. C. S.* III. pp. 366—465.)

1501, 1503, 1507. W. Smyth. (See for two of these his *Life*, by Churton, pp. 116—127. Cf. *L. C. S.* III. pp. 678—684.)

1515. W. Atwater.

1525. J. Longland.

[1536. Oct. 21. Meeting of leaders of the 'Pilgrimage of Grace.']

1552. J. Tayler.

1556. 1 Aug. J. White, pending Card. Pole's Visitation. White's Injunctions, Strype, *Memorials*, iii. Documents no. 52, *in fine*.

1607. W. Chaderton. (See *L. C. S.* III. p. 641.)

(Cir. 1617—21, G. Montaigne intends to visit.)

1664. B. Laney. (See *L. C. S.* III. pp. 644, 652.)

1679 (1690, through a Commission). T. Barlow.

1693. T. Tenison.

1696, 1697, 1700, 1703. James Gardiner.

1706, 1709, 1712. W. Wake. Also in 1715 by a Commission. (See *L. C. S.* III. pp. 647, 667, 669.)

1718. Edm. Gibson. (See *L. C. S.* III. pp. 647 foll.)

1724, 1729, 1733, 1736. Ri. Reynolds. (See *L. C. S.* III. pp. 647, 670.)

1745, 1748, 1751 (and 1755). J. Thomas.

[1871. Lincoln Diocesan Synod held in the Chapter-House.]

1873, 1876, 1879—80. Chr. Wordsworth. (See the first of his *Twelve Addresses*, and his *Statuta Eccl. Linc.* 1873. Also his *Diocesan Addresses*, 1876, p. 97, and *Ten Addresses*, 1879, p. 1. See also *L. C. S.* III. pp. 673—694.)

There are records of many of the above-mentioned Visitations among the Chapter Muniments, D. vi. 2. It is probable that there was an exception made to the Bishop of Lincoln's visitatorial right, viz. in the case of the prebendal parishes. See *L. C. S.* III. p. 282, *margin*, where Bp Alnwick keeps the question open for further consideration.

In comparatively early times the absolute right of a Bishop of *Salisbury* to visit his Chapter was successfully resisted by the Canons. In 1262 Egidius de Bridport,

who came from the deanery of Wells, and who had seen the Church of New Sarum completed, gave notice of his intention to visit the Dean and Chapter. When they challenged his authority in such a case, the Bishop examined into the matter, and confessed that he could not justify his claim, and testified in writing that the D. and C. of Salisbury were 'always free from visitation by Bishops of Sarum; particularly as we understand that this right belongs to the duty and dignity of the Dean.' It was a transcript of the document setting forth this Sarum privilege, that Dean Macworth at Lincoln procured as a weapon of defence against his Bishop[1]. But the Dean and Chapter of Salisbury in the 15th century did not inform the Lincoln folk that Pope Boniface IX. had shorn them considerably of this liberty. John Waltham, Bp of Sarum in 1392, had again claimed visitatorial jurisdiction and had brought their predecessors to a composition which the Pope confirmed. The Bishop gained for *himself* the right to visit *as often as he pleased*, and exercised it in 1393 (nearly the last year of his life), while he secured for his successors, Bishops of Salisbury, the right to visit the Dean and Chapter in the Chapter-House once every seven years. Thus Mr Rich Jones records three episcopal Visitations of Salisbury Cathedral in the 14th century, six in the latter half of the 15th, and four in the 17th century, the last being by Gilbert Burnet in 1697. In the time of Burnet's predecessor, Bp Seth Ward, Abp Sancroft, as well as Lord North, had been called to intervene when this right was disputed

[1] See the Lincoln *Black Book*, *L. C. S.* I. pp. 404—7; 165—6. We find nevertheless numerous later precedents for Visitation of Salisbury Cathedral Church by Bishops of Sarum, viz. in the years 1393, 1408, 1454, 1468, 1507 (misprinted '1570'), 1562, 1568, 1573, 1578, 1593, 1636, 1661, 1672, 1697: the first of these by Bp J. Waltham, the last by Gilbert Burnet. See Jones' *Fasti Sarisb.* p. 213. And still more recently the late Bishop of Salisbury visited the D. and C., Apr. 13th and 17th, 1888. See *Sarum Dio. Gazette*, pp. 22, 39. And cf. p. 110, at Oct. 30. About 1338 a Bishop of Wells visited his Cathedral Church, but not without some opposition.

in 1683—6; and the Primate succeeded in restoring concord by a Commission[1].

There is evidence that the Dean and Chapter of Lincoln have been visited by the Bishop of the Diocese on many occasions from the 13th century to the 19th.

As regards administration of the see when the bishopric was vacant, it appears that R. de Hayles, archdeacon of Lincoln, made institutions in the first year of St Edmund of Canterbury, i.e. in 1234—5, after the death of Hugh de Welles. (D. ii. 62, box 1.) After the death of Grosseteste, Abp Boniface claimed to administer the see, but W. Lupus, archd. of Lincoln, and the Chapter pleaded ancient custom for their jurisdiction. The evidence in favour of the Dean and Chapter of Lincoln, as well as the Articles put forward by the Primate, are preserved in a parchment book (D. ii. 62, no. 4) covered in a piece of a papal bull, 1253. The Abp took exception to some of the witnesses put forward by the D. and C., such as the late precentor, Peter de Audenham or Aldham, Michael, archd. of Bucks, and Walter de St Quentin, archd. of Taunton. (D. ii. 62, box 1.) A roll of about the same date, containing precedents from the dioceses of London, Canterbury, &c., in favour of the liberties of the D. and C. during vacancy of the see, is likewise preserved at Lincoln. (D. ii. 62, box 2.)

Even at the present day it has been allowed that of common right, as also by the canon law, Deans and Chapters are guardians of the spiritualities during a vacancy (as the king has custody of the temporalities). This still has the force of custom as regards the D. and C. of Canterbury, when the primatial see is vacant; but, either by prescription or by composition, the Archbishop claims in most other dioceses to execute all episcopal rights and to execute all ecclesiastical jurisdiction personally or by his Commissioners. (Burn, *Eccl. Law*, I. 225—6.) In

[1] *Fasti Eccl. Sar.*, W. H. [Rich] Jones, pp. 211—214. Instances of the Bp of Salisbury taking his place at Chapter meetings in the 16th—18th century are cited, *ibid.* p. 208 *n.*

the cases of Lincoln and Salisbury (and possibly of other dioceses) the Archbishop of Canterbury is bound to nominate one of the gremial Canons as his *officialis sede vacante*; but sometimes a Canon of Canterbury has acted as Vicar-General (circ. 1660)[1].

A mid-thirteenth century precedent for a large Chapter meeting or convocation of Canons at Lincoln (including, no doubt, a majority of Canons not at the moment 'in residence') is found among our muniments (D. ii. 60, box 2, labelled 'Internal Relations of Dean and Chapter: Vacancy of See'). Besides an earlier monition (1183—5) and many of a later period, there are seven documents here relating to the vacancy of the see which occurred after the death of Rob. Grosseteste, 9 Oct. 1253, his successor Dean H. de Lexington being elected Bishop 30 Dec. 1253, and consecrated 17 May 1254 by Abp Boniface *in partibus transmarinis*. Some of these records will be mentioned presently.

The disputes relating to jurisdiction and fees during the vacancy were not terminated until some time after the see had once again become vacant, and had been once more re-filled by the election of Ri. de Gravesend (who, like his predecessor H. de Lexington, had been dean), 30 Sept. 1258.

One of the documents in this box is a decision of Pope Alexander IV. judging all prebendaries to be liable with D. and C. to payment of contributions in defence of the liberties of the Church. This is dated 15 May 1256. Of other documents from D. ii. 60, box 2, we may mention in particular an Agreement (21 May 1261) between the Archbishop and the D. and C. of Lincoln about exercise of jurisdiction during the vacancy of the see, when it was settled that the Chapter should select

[1] The Abp is required to select one out of 'trȩs vel quatuor de Canonicis ipsius ecclesie' by the terms of the composition between Abp Boniface and the D. and C. made in 1261. *Black Book*, pp. 311—312. Precedents for *Lincoln* are found in 1299, 1319, 1705, &c. For *Salisbury* see their *Statutes* (ed. Dayman and Jones), pp. 19, 20.

three or four names from among the Canons, and that the Archbishop of Canterbury should nominate one of these as Official *sede vacante.* The see was already filled by the appointment of Bp Gravesend in 1258, but past difficulties had occasioned this arrangement with a view to future vacancies.

The remaining document, to which we are calling special attention, is of rather earlier date than the one just named. It is somewhat torn, but I give the writing which remains.

A Meeting of Bishop (or Dean) H.
with (Archdeacons and) Brethren
of Lincoln, about forty
in number, *in Capitulo*
14 Octob. [cir. 1255.]

MEMORANDUM quod pridie Idus Octobris, die scil*icet* sancti Kalixti, in Capitulo Linc*oln'* presen*tibus* dño H[enrico (de Lexynton) episcopo (? decano) Li]nc*oln'* et fratribus aliis quadraginta: Archidiaconi eiusdem ecclesie profitebantur quod, cum uacante sede Lincoln*iensi* Archidiaconi sunt in possessione [...*torn*...]os ad ecclesias parochiales de confirmand*o* electos · quod hanc possessionem habent et exercent iure et r*acio*ne Decani et Ca[pituli,] ad quos de iure Communi Iurediccio Episcopalis uacante sede dinoscitur pertinere. Ita tamen quod contra consuetudinem antiq*ua*m et optentam ipsis Decano et Capitulo super dictos Archidiaconos tempore uacacionis aliqua iurisdiccio non accrescat · [ubi] in casu [appellacionis] quantum ad expedicionem premissorum [...*torn*...] Archidiaconi concesserunt · vt q*ui*a materia q*ue*stionis mouebatur Decano et Capitulo super premissis Dño Bonefacio tunc Cantuar*iensi* Archiep[iscopo] super Jurisdiccione Episcopali predicta: Due partes sequestrorum que prouenerint in diocesi tempore uacacionis post obitum uenerabilis patris Dñi Roberti [nuper] Lincolñ Episcopi Capitulo per manus ipsorum Archidiaconorum assignentur. Et si causa proteletur ultra tempus quo

[prouisum] fuerit ecclesie Linc', dabunt integram partem ipsos contingentem dicto Capitulo · quousque causa fuerit terminata. Ita quidem quod huiusmodi [contribu]cio (? *al.* 'assignacio') Archidiaconis nullum preiudicium faciat, nec aliquo modo traheretur ad consequenciam in contribucionibus aliis futuris temporibus faciendis.

E[t in huius rei testimonium] huic scripto sigillum Capituli est ape*n*sum † vna cum sigillis Archidiaconorum ecclesie Li[ncolniensis].

(There are nine slits at the foot of the parchment through which the seals were probably attached, but only the middle one, probably that of the Dean and Chapter, has its shred of vellum remaining, and no crumb of wax is left adhering to it. The eight Archdeacons in Lincoln diocese at that time were those of Lincoln, Hunts, Northants, Leicester, Oxon, Bucks, Beds, and Stow.)

It will be seen that when in May 1261 Abp Boniface delivered his agreement or 'composition' at Lambeth, between himself and the Dean and Chapter of Lincoln (*Black Book*, pp. 311—315), it was determined that the Archdeacons should have one third part of the *sequestra* which would have accrued to the Bishop had the see been filled up, in addition to their usual share. The Archdeacon of Bucks in any case received *all* sequestrations gathered in his own Archdeaconry. They were also to have one quarter of the synodal contributions. The Archbishop was to take the remainder of the Bishop of Lincoln's dues *cum onere suo*. We have quoted (*ibid.* p. 88) another curious relic of the same dispute, namely, the Dean's letter to the Subdean, to which we will presently refer.

We may conclude that the meeting of the 'forty Brethren' *in Capitulo*[1] took place in the October of 1254

[1] '*Greater Chapter*': so says J. F. Wickenden's memorandum in D. ii. 60, box 2. But I suppose Bradshaw would not approve the phrase. In point of fact no such phrase is used in the document itself, but only 'presente dn̄o' &c. 'et fratribus aliis quadraginta.' Wickenden in describing the document merely used a phrase which a dozen years ago was

or of some other year not later than 1260, after which the dispute was at an end; and most probably before Aug. 1258 when H. de Lexington died. Possibly it may have been dated as early as 14 Oct. 1253: in which case we must supply 'dño H[enrico de Lexyngton *Decano* Lin]coln'.'

Very early in the time of Bp Gravesend we find the D. and C. calling in the assistance of the Pope (Alexander IV.) to repel the invasion of their rights by the Abp of *York* (Godfrey de Ludham). His bull, dated 24 Apr. 1259, may be seen at Lincoln, with four other documents somewhat later; two protests, made in the time of Oliver Sutton, against the officials of the Court of J. Peckham, Abp of Canterbury, attempting to administer wills, &c., 23 Feb. 1280, 1 Feb. 1290; and a notice of appeal is dated 1 May 1291. A notarial instrument for J. de Dalderby complains of some interference with his right to appoint to all prebends of Lincoln, 25 Sept. 1312[1].

After the death of Henry de Lexington, 8 Aug. 1258, although the temporalities were restored to his successor, Richard de Gravesend, about two months later[2], the Archbishop found time to attempt the exercise of jurisdiction[3]. On the 24th of Aug. 1258 the Pope issued an Injunction restraining the Archbishop from promulgating excommunications in the diocese of Lincoln during the vacancy. We have a memorandum of the protest made by two of the Canons (J. Derby and W. de Hemyngburgh) on the part of the D. and C. In the month of October (1258) the precentor Hugh, and John, Chancellor of

'in the air.' (See *Lincoln Cathedral Statutes*, II. pp. cii, clxxxiv *n.*, III. 707—9.)

[1] All these are in D. ii. 62, box 1.

[2] The election no doubt was hurried on, because K. Henry III. was taking steps to get a nominee of his own appointed, viz. Peter de Aqua Blanca, Bp of Hereford, who did not bear a good repute with churchmen, as he had been guilty of a fraudulent act.

[3] There was, I believe, an early claim made (on the death of Grosseteste in 1253) by the same Abp Boniface to administer the diocese. Evidence for D. and C. of Lincoln. Articles advanced by Abp Boniface may be found in our Muniment Room, D. ii. 62 (box 4). This is a parchment book of 35 (formerly 43) leaves and has a papal bull for its cover.

York, served a monition upon Abp Boniface, requiring him (under authority of a bull of Alexander IV., 2 Nov. 1254) not to subject the D. and C. of Lincoln to ecclesiastical censures while defending the rights of their Church. The dispute, as we have seen, was not settled until 22 May 1261[1], and there is a trace of its progress after the new Bishop's consecration in the letter of Dean R. de Marisco (23 Aug. 1259) to the Subdean, asking him to forward evidences, which I have given in the previous volume[2].

Instances of Metropolitical Visitation of the diocese of Lincoln by Archbishops of Canterbury may be cited :—

The Latin verses cited (from MS. Y at Chichester) in the *Hist. MSS. Commission Report*, 8vo, I. p. 189 (1901), imply that Abp J. Peckham visited Lincoln among other dioceses in his six years' course, cir. 1285—90.

1320. Walter Reynold.

J. Gynwell, Bp of Lincoln, procured a bull of exemption at great cost from Pope Clement VI. It was, however, set aside in favour of the claims put forward by Abp Islip.

1390. W. Courtenay. (See A. 2. 11, no. 2.)

1505, June 18, 19. W. Warham's Vicar-General. (See portfolio A. 3. 19, among Chapter Acts.)

1556. Reginald Pole, Cardinal Abp.

1602. J. Whitgift.

1634. W. Laud (by his Vicar-General)[3].

1673. Gilb. Sheldon.

1686. W. Sancroft.

In Apr. 1548 the Royal Visitors of K. Edward VI. sent Injunctions to Lincoln. (See *L. C. S.* III. pp. 579, 583—596.)

In 1559 Q. Elizabeth held a Royal Visitation by Commissioners.

It has been remarked that the Dean, being required

[1] *Black Book*, pp. 311—315.

[2] *Black Book*, pp. 88, 89. The original, with the other documents mentioned in the context above, are in D. ii. 60, box 2.

[3] Laud reports to the king that Lincoln Cathedral 'is not well ordered, either for reparation or ornaments; but the Dean and Chapter, to whom that care belongs, have promised speedy amendment.' Wharton's *Hist. of Tryals*, I. p. 531, ed. 1695.

by statute to be constantly present, is rather a perpetual *supervisor* than an occasional *visitor*. He had, however, at Lincoln (to quote a passage from an address given by my Father, when Bishop of Lincoln, to the Chapter in 1873) "the cure of souls of all the members of the capitular body. He had archidiaconal jurisdiction in all the parishes annexed to the prebends of the Cathedral. He was the 'Censor morum' of the whole body, and all its members promised obedience to him.

"In some Cathedrals of the old foundation [as at Lichfield] the Dean exercised archidiaconal jurisdiction over the churches and parishes of the Cathedral city. This does not appear to have been the case at Lincoln [where even in Bp Grosseteste's time, A.D. 1240, there was a 'Rural Dean of *Christianity*'...subordinate to the Archdeacon of Lincoln]; but he had the right of visiting the Chapter triennially, and of correcting abuses in it[1]."

Also "at Lincoln he (the Dean) had the cure of souls in the precincts, and of all that large body of persons who were engaged in the services of the Cathedral Church." Modern changes have left him "without a parish as well as without an archdeaconry[2]."

We find several Deans of Lincoln holding their Visitations[3], as of old (*L. C. S.* II. p. civ, III. p. 288), so in modern times:—

[1] *Twelve Addresses delivered at his Visitation* of the Cathedral and Diocese of Lincoln, A.D. 1873, *by* Chr. Wordsworth, D.D., *Bp of Lincoln*, pp. 12, 13.

[2] *Ibid.* p. 25. *Lincoln Cathedral Statutes*, III. pp. 285, 342—3; 422 § 26.

[3] I have not yet read the records of Decanal Visitations, but I find that in Feb. 1322 the Subdean and Chapter assured Dean Mammesfeld that *Chapter* as well as Dean ought to issue summons for his Visitation. It was held in St Mary Magdalen's Church; continued 27 Apr. 1322. Visitations of Prebendal estates and Churches and their dependent Chapels by Deans of *Sarum* in 1220, 1222, 1224, and 1226 are recorded in the 'Osmund' Register, and the duty of the Dean to visit prebends in case the Canons were negligent, was established by an ordinance or constitution of the year 1214 passed when Ri. Poore was Dean of Sarum and Rob. Grosseteste Archdeacon of Wilts. The Dean of *Westminster* used to go on 'progress' round the Chapter estates holding his courts

1663, 1666, 1669, 1673, 1676. Michael Honywood. (His monition is in D. vii. 2, no. 20.)

1698. Sam. Fuller.

1737. E. Willes (D. ii. 55, box 3).

1791. Sir Ri. Kaye.

For two hundred years after Grosseteste's time[1], when internal troubles arose at Lincoln, in spite of the founder's efforts to place his Canons out of the hearing of the strife of tongues, and 'ab omni garrulitatis cuiuslibet strepitu liberos,' the Bishop was able to exercise his proper function, as peacemaker, from a position of superiority, and as a general rule to turn to good account that intimate knowledge of the unwritten customs with which his apprenticeship as a prebendary had endowed him, and which for the most part (when faithfully and wisely applied) met with a loyal submission from the contending parties.

These were the Deans from time to time and certain of the Canons[2]: and during the period which we have indicated the *lauda episcoporum*, or awards, were pretty numerous. But within this time, if a Bishop ever figures as a party in the dispute, it is not the Bishop of the diocese—his position is clearly established—but it is the

and visiting the Churches in modern times. Thus I have seen the itinerary note-book of his progress, with rapid sketches in his own hand, by Samuel Wilberforce, made when he was Dean in 1846.

[1] In the Chapter Acts '*A. primum*' (A. 2. 22) there is a single sheet which contains the proceedings of the Chancellor Ralph Barry, the Subdean H. de Beningworth, and J. de Harington, who had been appointed Commissioners in Chapter in 1312—13, in the question between Dean Roger de Martiuallis (so the name is there spelt uniformly) and the Canons. The sittings were carried on to Whitsun-eve, 2 June, 1313. J. de Schalby's and A. de Beek's books speak of other quarrels.

[2] John de Schalby, in his brief memoirs of the Bishops of Lincoln, records that among Grosseteste's papers were found after his death several bulls which he had procured for the protection of his episcopal rights, and that with these was preserved the bull *Attendentes* of Innocent IV., A.D. 1252, by which the clergy were excused and exempted from paying procuration-fees to the Archbishop when he held a Metropolitical Visitation. See *Liber Niger*, p. 323, *Schalby's Book*, lf. 5ª. There is at Lincoln a letter of Innocent IV. (31 Oct. anno 1°, 1243) on the Appeal of the D. and C. against the right of the Bishop to visit in the Chapter-House and in Prebendal Churches. D. ii. 62, box 1.

Primate of all England, or else the Pope of Rome, who intervenes or appears as a party to some suit. Thus we find, in 1261, Boniface Abp of Canterbury issuing an Award, or Composition, between himself and Rob. de Mariscis (Dean) and Chapter of Lincoln and their respective successors to provide for the exercise of jurisdiction in the interval between the decease or cession of a Bishop of Lincoln and the admission of his successor. Some difficulties may have arisen on occasion of the last vacancy previous, i.e. between the death of Henry de Lexington and the appointment of Richard de Gravesend. Both these prelates had themselves been Deans of Lincoln, as was Oliver Sutton when the next vacancy occurred in Dec. 1279. In 1333—4 Pope John XXII. intervened in the days of Bp H. de Burghersh, Ant. Beek the younger being Dean, who bequeathed the suit at Avignon, probably to his immediate successor John de Nottingham, and certainly to W. Bateman ('de Norwich') who succeeded to the Deanery in 1340. The Bishop of Lincoln was not a party to this suit, but the dispute lay between the Dean for the time being and the Chapter. In 1346 Abp J. Stratford gave a decision in the matter of the appointment to the keepership of the Altar of St Peter, which was in dispute between J. de Ufford and the Chapter. Here again the Bishop, Thomas le Bek, was not a party to the suit excepting so far as he might be considered to have a small share in the prebendal right involved. J. de Ufford had been prebendary *centum solidorum* before he exchanged into the Chapter of St Paul's.

Several documents of this date remain at Lincoln (in D. ii. 60, box 2). The following may be enumerated.

The Chapter of Lincoln revoke the mandate of J. de Bourne, prebendary of Bedford major, their proctor in a suit brought against them by J. de Nottingham, the late Dean, and W. Bateman de Norwich, his successor, 30 Apr. 1341.—Decision of Abp J. Stratford on appeal of Dean Bateman and Simon de Islip, preb. of Welton Beckhall, on behalf of the Chapter, appearing personally,

on the rights of the Dean and the Chapter respectively, 9 Mar. 1343.—Decision of Abp Stratford on matters in dispute between Dean Bateman and the Chapter, cir. 1340—4.

Nic. Vordis, LL.D., papal auditor, writes to [T. Arundel] Abp, declaring the relative jurisdiction of the Dean of Lincoln and the Chapter, at the instance of J. de Shepey, Dean, 1407.—Appeal against Dean Shepey. The Subdean and Chapter at a Visitation of the Chapter make representation concerning the inconvenience caused by non-residence of the Dean (no date or name given. But we state that Shepey was the Dean in question on Bradshaw's authority). (D. ii. 60, box 2.)

Bp John de Dalderby had had a dispute with Robert Winchelsey, Abp of Canterbury (cir. 1300—13), as to the right of probate of the wills of such persons as died possessed of property in the diocese of Lincoln and elsewhere. A suit was pending in the Court of Rome; but the next Archbishop, Walter Reynold, came to terms with the Bishop (8 Jan. 1319) out of court, and agreed to renounce all right of appeal upon the question, as may be seen in the *Black Book*, pp. 324—5. Two days earlier the Primate had confirmed the rights of the Dean and Chapter in various churches. (D. ii. 62, box 1.)

In 1390 we find W. Courtenay, Abp of Canterbury, holding a Visitation; it is thought that he considered the worthy old Bishop of Lincoln, John de Bokingham, scarcely zealous enough in his enquiry after the Lollards or Wycliffites in his diocese, and he had accordingly visited him at Leicester in 1389. A copy of his ordinance on disorders in the Cathedral Church at Lincoln, 12 May, 1390, in a late 15th cent. transcript, is preserved among the muniments in the portfolio marked A. 2. 11.

In 1388 John de Shepey, LL.D., Chancellor of Lichfield 1368—76, succeeded to the Deanery of Lincoln. Complaints were raised by the Chapter against his administration, and the cause was tried and decided by an award, in 1404, by Henry Beaufort, then Bishop of the

diocese of Lincoln and subsequently Bishop of Winchester and Cardinal[1].

In 1412 John Macworth, LL.D., succeeded to the Deanery. He had been Chancellor to Henry Prince of Wales (afterwards King Henry V.), and in 1404 was presented by the King, Henry IV., to the stall of Empingham in Lincoln Minster (his brother, Thomas Mackworth of Mackworth in co. Derby, having, as Mr Maddison informs us, married the heiress of that manor). Under such patronage, and being a man of considerable force of character, he maintained his right to this prebend against a nominee of Pope Innocent VII., although it was not until the year of his appointment to the Deanery that he received installation. In the interim he had been Archdeacon of Dorset (1406) and of Norfolk (1408). In 1422 Bp Richard Flemmyng collated him to the stall of Nassington, which he held until his death in 1451. While he was Dean of Lincoln he saw a succession of five or six Bishops. Philip Repingdon (who had been abbat of Leicester and Chancellor of Oxford in 1400, and Cardinal in 1408) resigned his see in 1419, as King Henry V. had set his face against English Bishops receiving the hat. Richard Flemmyng succeeded. Then in 1431 William Gray, who had been Dean of York 1421, and Bp of London 1426. William Alnwick, who was translated from Norwich in 1436. And, lastly, Marmaduke Lumley, translated from Carlisle, who held the see for some months only in 1450. John Chedworth, though elected early in 1451, was not consecrated till June 1452; and in this interval Dean Macworth died, after holding the Deanery for nearly forty years.

Under four Bishops, and for the space of about five and twenty years, Dean Macworth was constantly delated to the Bishop for the time being, by several of the Canons, on charges somewhat similar to those for which his predecessor J. de Shepeye had been censured. Year after

[1] The Chapter had also a dispute with the Treasurer (prob. Peter Dalton) about 1388. A paper of evidence on the subject is in A. 2. 13.

year he had enjoyed his prebend in Rutland (or, after 1422, in Northamptonshire), his non-residence being in itself a scandal; but he never would consent to provide a vicar according to the statute 'to follow the choir in place of the absent canon.' He received (so the charges alleged against him) the rents of Chesterfield mill, and of property at Worksworth and Querenden, but he persistently neglected to fulfil the obligation for which these endowments had been left, or to provide a chaplain to pray for his predecessors' and other Christian souls at the *missa matutinalis*. He neglected the celebration of obits of kings and bishops, for which he was bound to provide. He would not entertain the ministers of the Cathedral upon double feasts, as the statutes required him to do. He required persons to attend him at a distance from their homes, and in unstatutable places. He told scandalous tales about the canons to personages in high station. When he came to Lincoln he did not behave more acceptably:—he made the ringers stop the bells before the canon on duty could arrive at the church, he sent word to the choir to wait out for him to come to mass long after the celebrant had gone to the altar. He claimed to say mass in place of the regular celebrant at a moment's notice. He introduced into the Chapter-House armed laymen to overawe the Chapter, and a clerk to tell the secrets of their deliberations. His servants kept the close-gates open at improper hours, and interfered with the porter in the performance of his duty. The Dean took away the 'Black Book,' which ought to be left for reference in the church. This last was a special offence, because this 'liber consuetudinarius ecclesie' was, in those days of litigation, liable to be required as an evidence; and we find instances as early as the time of J. de Schalby and as late as the 17th and 18th centuries when books of Lincoln Statutes and Customs were exhibited in court. Some of these charges may have been trivial and spiteful, others may have been due to a desire of certain offenders to hide their own shady character by blackening the

reputation of another. But I can hardly suppose that all were without foundation in fact.

Bishop after bishop was entreated to intervene, and the Dean of Lincoln treated them somewhat as in later days Dr Bentley treated the Bishop of Ely and the University authorities; except that Macworth did not appeal to any other tribunal, but made repeated protestations of his willingness to abide by his lordship's decree. Cardinal Repyngdon and Bp Flemmyng both tried their hands at a composition between the parties, but with no permanent success. Then Bp Gray produced an excellent award, but unfortunately he or his legal advisers had not been sufficiently business-like in the preliminaries, and (as in the case of so many of the ecclesiastical judgments in a recent generation) a slight flaw upset the whole.

We may pause in this place to give the preamble of Bp Gray's *Laudum* (24—27 Sept. 1434) and to enumerate the counter-charges which the Dean brought against the Canons[1].

In Dei Nomine Amen.

Cum post Laudum dudum super diuersis[2] et discordiis inter magistrum Johannem Macworth decanum ecclesie Lincolñ et Capitulum eiusdem exortis latum, nonnulle alie graues discordie, lites, et dissenciones inter eosdem Decanum et Capitulum, inimico homini, qui zizania superseminauit[3], ministrante, denuo sunt exorte,

[1] We owe these extracts to the kindness of the Rev. A. R. Maddison, F.S.A.

[2] *diuersis*: Anglicè, 'differences.'

[3] This reminds us of the phrase in Alnwick's *Novum Registrum*, 'procurante satore zizannie, qui iugiter sedet in insidiis ecclesiasticis viris,' where he is quoting Bp Braybrooke, and *he* imitating the *Corpus Juris Canonici*. See *L. C. S.* III. p. 269. I recognise the first part of this phrase in Abp Kempe's Injunctions for Windsor in 1432; and the latter half has a parallel in one of the Canons of the Council of Oxford which are sometimes cited as of the year 1222. 'Quia vero nonnumquam serpens antiquus, qui iugiter insidiatur sanctis viris' (*Provinc.* app. p. 5), where

Ad quas penitus cedendas† pacemque inter ipsos Decanum et Capitulum componendam ac reformandos mores in populo,

Nos Will'mus permissione diuina Lincolñ episcopus prefatos Dec. et Cap., singulosque Canonicos dicte ecclesie nostre Lincolñ, ac alios dignitates, prebendas, personatus vel officia in eadem obtinentes, et infra Regnum protunc existentes &c.

in domo capitulari dicte ecclesie nostre Lincolñ fecimus conuocari.

In cuiusmodi conuocacione nostra[1] dictus magister Johannes decanus nonnullas materias litis, controuersie, et discordie inter ipsum et dictum Capitulum exortarum quamplura querelas et grauamina sibi et dignitati sue decanali, vt asseruit, multum preiudicialia, et per dictum Cap. sibi, vt eciam asseruit, illata et irrogata continentes, videlicet,

1. de medietate feodorum &c. per Canonicos subtracta per sex annos contra laudum.

2. de approbacione et insinuacione testamentorum infra clausum Lincolñ &c.

3. de confirmacione cartarum &c.

4. de presentacione ad ecclesias et vicarias &c.

5. de iurisdiccione exercitata per Canonicos sub nomine Capituli in commorantes in prebendis extra Ciuitatem Lincolñ, contra laudum.

6. de obligacione ecclesie Lincolñ pro obitu Ricardi Rauenser et Will'i Waltham tenendo[2] absque consensu

Spelman's text (ii. p. 188) has 'jugiter *sedet in insidiis* sanctis viris.' It seems probable that Bp Gray (as we find to be the case perhaps with Gravesend before—see *Black Book*, pp. 419—420—and Alnwick after him, *Lincoln Cathedral Statutes*, III. pp. 268 *n.*, 496) used the phraseology of the canonists in his awards as naturally and unconsciously as their modern successors would adopt biblical phraseology in their sermons and addresses.

[1] The use of the term *Conuocacio nostra* by Bp Alnwick's predecessor should be observed.

[2] In the 14th century *Liber Cantariarum*, the Ordinance for the Chantry of J. Ravenser (20 Aug. 1398), inserted at lf. 187[b], 188[a], provides that two chaplains should dwell in one lodging, or at all events both within the close. They are to wear the choral habit and to take part

decani per Canonicos facta, et de sexcentis marcis receptis pro eadem per dictos Canonicos, cuius summe magnam partem suis usubus ceperunt.

7. de firmis canonicalibus destructis &c.

8. de cantariis in ecclesia Lincolñ contra earum fundacionem et ordinacionem vnitis[1], et earum co*m*modis et emolumentis per Canonicos in eorum usus perceptis, suffragiis pro animabus fundatorum omissis.

9. de alienacione temporalium ecclesie Lincolñ per Canonicos &c.

10. de distribucione facienda inter pauperes ciuitatis Lincolñ pro anima fundatoris cantarie de Burghersshe &c.[2]

11. de centum libris pro reparacione tenementorum fabrice ecclesie Lincolñ, et centum marcis pro reparacione firmarum eiusdem ecclesie per magistrum Petrum Dalton relictis &c.[3]

12. Et de vendicione et alienacione perpetua calicum a*n*nulorum et aliorum iocalium ecclesie Lincolñ per canonicos uenditorum &c.

The heads of the Canons' complaints against the Dean,

in processions: not to keep a tavern or to frequent dicings (*taxillos*), but to avoid loose company. Their duty was to celebrate for K. Richard (II.), Henry (Beaufort) Bp, Edw. Duke of Albemarle, Eustachia de Ravenser, prioress of Stykeswold, J. Ravenser Canon, Richard Ravenser Archd. of Linc. *ob.* May 1386, W. de Waltham canon preb. of Carlton Kyme, *ob.* 1418. (Ric. de Ragenhill, rector of Werpleston Wynton, and J. de Popilton, rector of Parkbrimpton, York, executors.) This chantry was founded at St Nicholas' altar 1374–5 (D. ii. 50, box 2). Richard Ravenser gave a cope of white cloth of gold to the Minster. John de Ravenser became preb. of Castor (exchanging from Hovedon) in 1387. He died in 1393, but I think that Hardy is confusing John with Richard when he calls him (*Fasti*, p. 126) 'archdeacon.' Both of them held prebends at York.

1 On the Union of small Chantries, see *Lincoln Cathedral Statutes*, III. pp. 201, 439.

2 The Ordinance of the Burghersh Chantry is in the *Liber Cantariarum*, fo. 334 *bis*.

3 Philip Dalton, treasurer of Lincoln, died in Nov. 1402 (?) and was buried in the nave. He gave to the Minster a pair of silver candlesticks, a blue cope, and a green cope.

of which the full text is given below, are thus introduced:—

Prefatum quoque Capitulum eciam nonnullas materias litis, controuersie, et discordie inter ipsum Capitulum et dictum magistrum Johannem Decanum exortarum quamplura querelas et grauamina ipsi Capitulo, et quibusdam singularibus personis eiusdem, ut pars dicti Capituli asseruit, multum preiudicialia et damnosa, &c.

1. De non residencia et diuturna absencia ipsius Decani ab ecclesia.

2. De pastu chori in festis principalibus, absente Episcopo, per Decanum abstracto.

3. De intitulacione et tabulacione Decani ad supportand' omnia[1] in principalibus et aliis festis.

[1] *forsan* 'onera.'

4. De vicario per quemlibet Canonicum non residenciarium ecclesie per se in choro.

5. De septimis per quemlibet canonicum non residenciarium soluend' annuatim, per Dec. non residenciarium subtractis contra iuramentum suum.

6. De correccione detectorum in visitacione Episcopi per Dec. et Capitulum facienda, et per Dec. soli sibi vsurpata.

7. De monicionibus, citacionibus et mandatis auctoritate et nomine Decani et Capituli fiendis, et per Dec. solum suo nomine factis.

8. De Clerico suspecto Decani per ipsum in Capitulum introducto, per quem secreta Capituli reuelantur.

9. De medietate correccionum Canonicorum in Visitacione Decani, a dicto Cap. per Dec. detenta contra laudum.

10. De obediencia per Decanum ex*t*orta a quibusdam canonicis admissis, contra formam laudi et preter voluntatem et reclamacionem Canonici.

11. De distribucionibus solum inter Canonicos Residenciarios faciendis, per Dec., Canonicum non residenciarium, contra laudabilem consuetudinem ecclesie [indebite] exactis et perceptis.

12. De Choristis per presidentem et Capitulum in

absencia Decani admissis, et per ipsum Dec., absque consensu Capituli, et absque causa racionabili, suspensis.

13. De Inordinato transitu Decani in processionibus contra solitam consuetudinem ecclesie in hoc obseruatam.

14. De Capellano, qui missam matutinalem intitulatus sumptibus Decani celebret[1], per ipsum Dec. non sustentato debite, sed subtracto.

15. De Seruientibus familiaribus Decani impedientibus Janitorem portarum Clausi, ne ipsas portas tempore debito claudere possit, contra consuet. ecclesie.

16. De Jurisdiccione per Decanum adempta a presidente et Capitulo in prebendis et prebendariis in absencia seu necligencia Decani, quam idem Dec. presens et Capitulum extra tempus visitacionis sue decanalis habent in eisdem, contra consuetudinem ecclesie.

17. De obitu Dñi Henr. Lexington per Decanum, vt in duabus marcis per ipsum soluendis tenendo per eundem Dec. subtracto contra Ordinacionem obitus huiusmodi[2].

18. De diminucione feodorum Clerici Capituli et Clerici scribentis litteras Induccionum.

19. De ·xiiij· libris mutuatis per Decanum de bonis communibus Capituli...et satisfaciend' ipsi Capitulo.

20. De quatuor libris restituendis Capitulo, quas Idem Decanus de bonis Capituli soluit pro contemptu, quem idem Dec. propria culpa meruit in [Curia] Cantuariensi.

21. De prohibicione per Decanum facta debitoribus solut' Capituli et non Decani [ne de]bita sua ipsi Capitulo soluant.

22. De eo quod Decanus euocat subditos infra prebendas commorantes ad loca [exteriora, et] trahit ad iudiccium extra tempus visitacionis sue decanalis, contra consuetudines et privilegia ecclesie.

[1] This Morrow Mass was founded in 1252 by Roger de Weseham (who had been Dean of Lincoln) when he was Bp of Lichfield. See *Ant. Beek's Book*, fo. 23. (*Lincoln Cathedral Statutes*, II. pp. lviii, lix.)

[2] Henry de Lexington Bp in 1260 founded a chantry for two priests at the altar of St John [Bapt.] where he was buried. *Chantry Book*, lf. 156[b], cf. 1[a]. His Obit ordered by Bp Gravesend and Chapter, *ibid.* lf. 12[a].

23. De eo quod Decanus Canonicos residenciarios, et alios habitum in Ecclesia [portant]es, ad loca remota extra clausum ecclesie euocat ad iudicium [et uoca]ri facit, contra consuetudinem ecclesie et tenorem laudi, penam inibi contentam incurrendo.

24. De familiaribus secularibus laicis Decani sedentibus infra domum Capitularem cum Armis inuasiuis, diebus Capitularibus, et in conuencionibus Decani et Canonicorum, contra consuetudinem ecclesie: cum vnus solus virgarius custodiret ostium Capituli.

25. De admissione pauperum clericorum per Decanum in hospicio suo, et extra Capitulum, et absque prestacione obediencie et iuramenti requisit', contra consuetudinem ecclesie facta.

26. De eo quod Decanus facit vltimam pulsacionem ad vesperas eciam † primam cessare ante aduentum executoris officij, contra consuetudinem ecclesie.

27. De mandato Decani vt chorus expectet aduentum suum, postquam executor officij inceperit missam suam, in magnum scandalum ecclesie.

28. De extorcionibus factis per Decanum de certis ministris ecclesie, ad solam suggestionem fam*ul*ar' Decani.

29. De ablacione libri Consuetudinarij, qui dicitur *niger liber*, ab ecclesia per Decanum, qui liber debet in ecclesia de eius consuetudine remanere.

30. De eo quod Decanus impedit Capitulum ne Capitulum corrigat delicta grauia in defectu ipsius Decani post trinam requisicionem Decani per Capitulum, iuxta formam laudi factam periurium incurrendo.

31. De priuacione et suspensione Vicariorum chori presentatorum per eorum patronos et per Capitulum, absente Decano, admissorum, per Decanum iuris ordine non seruato facta.

32. De eo quod Dec. iuxta laudum non vocat Canonicos ad sibi assidendum in correccionibus per eum faciendis, vel non expectat vocatos, aut eorum non requirit consilium, contra laudum, penam illius incurrendo.

33. De eo quod Dec. presens non celebrat nec facit

celebrari in obitibus Regum et Episcoporum, prout tenetur ex statutis et consuetudinibus ecclesie iuratis.

34. De subuersione laudabilis ordinis et regule Chori in festis solempnibus per Dec. facta, contra tabulacionem in hac parte factam, missas maiores ex impetu celebrando.

35. De diffamacione Capituli super adulterio et fornicacione per Dec. facta apud nobiles.

36. De quatuor libris receptis per Dec. de Fabrica Ecclesie pro reparacione hospicij sui, quas restituere renuit.

37. De eo quod Dec. plures prebendas in die, per se et procuratores suos, visitat, et totidem recipit integras et excessiuas procuraciones absque dispensacione penas Juris incurrendo *Diuisim ministrarunt*[1], et vt premittitur ministrauit vterque eorundem.

How fairly Bp W. Gray dealt with these cross-petitions the decision of his *laudum*, now in print[2], declares. It did not however meet with loyal acquiescence, and in Oct. 1435 the Dean and his retainers were called upon to answer in the Abp's court a charge of violence. Within two years after the award had been delivered Bp Gray died, and nearly another year had elapsed before his successor, then Bp of Norwich, was fully installed in the see of Lincoln, in Feb. 1437. Unfortunately he lacked the prestige of having been elected by the Chapter, his translation having been decreed by Pope Eugenius IV. This honour was not an exceptional thing, for St John de Dalderby in 1300 had been the last Bishop of Lincoln freely elected by the Chapter.

William Alnwick, the new Bishop, was a man of very different character from the Dean, though he was his equal in pertinacity. Like Macworth he had taken a law degree at Cambridge. He had also been Archdeacon of Salisbury and had held a prebend there and one at York. At Norwich, to which he was consecrated in 1426, he built the W. front of the Cathedral Church, and at Cambridge he contributed to the building of the schools. At Lincoln

[1] See *Lincoln Cathedral Statutes*, III. p. 266.

[2] *Id.* pp. 259—266.

he made the S. porch and inserted the W. windows. He also built a new chapel to the Bishop's Palace. His arms appear on the E. end of the Vicars' stables, and he granted to their community several parcels of land in and about Lincoln, with larger estates in other places. Some notion of his spiritual character and prudence may be gathered from the fact that so devout a monarch as K. Henry VI. chose him as his confessor.

Alnwick had not been a year at Lincoln ere the Dean and the Chapter brought their several grievances to him one against the other.

The Bishop visited his Cathedral Church Oct. 1—4, 6—8, 1437, and then complaints and recriminations poured in from every side from the Dean to the youngest chorister. An impartial account of the proceedings has been given by the succentor of Lincoln, the Rev. A. R. Maddison, F.S.A., in a paper read before the Archæological Institute 30 July 1889. Knowing what we do of the internal life of Lincoln, we do not hesitate to say that even in the lowest ebb of spiritual life in the latter years of King George III. or under the Regency, our Cathedral was in a less corrupt and unhealthy state than it was in the days when Bp Alnwick held his Visitations. In spite of our disgust at some of the methods and the tools of the Reformation in the sixteenth century, and notwithstanding our affection for the exquisite beauty of much which the men of that time destroyed, we are bound to admit in common honesty that an English Reformation was the only hope for the Church in Lincoln, and that so long as leave should of necessity be sought either at Rome alone, or in the Chapter as it then existed, for effecting any improvement worthy of consideration, nothing could be effectually done.

Our concern here present is not with charges of the graver kind, which were by no means lacking[1]. It is

[1] Of sensuality which were preferred against two or three of the Vicars (and one of the Residentiary Canons), some of whom were apparently incorrigible. It may be said that Lincoln was not worse in this respect than other Cathedrals in the 15th century in this or other

enough to point out the tottering state of 'a house divided against a house.'

Dean Macworth complained in 1437 that the Canons were confederate against him. He named six of them, Chancellor Partrich, Archdeacons Southam and Derby, Treasurer Haket or Haget, and Prebendaries Warde and Ingoldsby. These were all of them residentiaries; and it is clear that, reinforced by Precentor Burton, Archd. Lascelles, Subdean Percy, and Canon Marshall, they appeared as still opposed to the Dean in the renewed complaints, upwards of forty in number, which they brought to the Bishop in June 1438. (See below, pp. 56 ff.) In 1437, of the eight complaints brought by the Dean against the Canons, the 1st and 5th together correspond with the 5th of 1438 (p. 82), that the Canons, instead of providing chaplains of their own, draw off the best singers from choir and chantries to attend them. The other charges are additional. Two of the Archdeacons and the Chancellor talk in service time. Prebendaries Rolleston and Selby have not provided vicars. Archd. W. Derby is allowed to count as resident while he is engaged in a Chancery suit at Westminster on which he expends the common funds, so that stipends cannot be paid. Books are kept out of the library. Sufficient workmen are not employed (*L. C. S.* III. pp. 366—9). Precentor Burton complains likewise that every man's hand is against *him*; the majority of the Chapter kept back the emoluments due to the minority. The sacrist, J. Leeke, claims to hear general confessions throughout the diocese, although the bull which he holds says only *casus reservatos episcopo*, and he likewise holds 'incompatible' offices (*L. C. S.* III. pp. 369—373). Peter Partrich, the Chancellor, brings against the Dean in 1437 several of those complaints which figure in the Canons'

countries. J. Molanus writing a century later, about 1585, mentions how the righteous souls of three successive Deans of Louvain before his time had been vexed by several of the cathedral body there who were 'notorie incontinentes et quod peius est, incorrigibiles.' *De Canonicis* lib. 2, cap. 6.

articles of 1438 (see nos. 11, 32, 33, 38, pp. 60—64; cf. *L. C. S.* III. pp. 374—5), including the matters of the Dean's stables, Bp Gray's award, the key of the seal, irregular walking in procession with (or close behind) the celebrant, and that curious question with which Bp Alnwick attempted to deal in the *Novum Registrum* (*Ibid.* p. 397), the Dean's train (*caudam cape sue*) being borne outside the close or in the Bishop's presence. The origin of this last item, though the matter is trivial, is worth noting. It is clear that this matter affecting the Dean's dignity, about which Macworth declared himself to be sorely aggrieved, was not raised by the new Bishop himself, but by one of the senior Canons, who may be supposed to have been well versed in Lincoln customs. W. Derby, Archd. of Bedford, corroborated what the Chancellor had said about the Dean's cope, and further charged Macworth with having brought armed men into the choir in the presence of a large congregation at evensong on 28th June 1435, committing assault and battery, with indignity, upon the Chancellor (*Ibid.* pp. 380—1)[1]. Several of the Canons complain that Treasurer Haget has spent his money upon feasting and amusements, instead of providing tapers at the Bishops' tombs, and on the beams north and south of the high altar. The Treasurers in return, and others likewise, report that many vicars and poor clerks slip out of choir during mass, or at mattins after *Venite*, and then return from taverns, or from gossiping in nave and close, just in time for the conclusion of Lauds. The Subdean says that the vergers do not enforce silence during sermons. The vicars, who were visited by Ro. Thornton, the Bishop's Commissary, corroborated the charges against some of the Canons, adding that Precentor Burton has pulled down two churches and appropriated the materials. There is much immorality among Canons and others, and some gambling. The revenues are wasted on law-suits, while books and vestments are needing repair, and stipends are in arrears. John Bellrynger keeps a

[1] On this outrage in choir, see also *Lincoln Cathedral Statutes*, II. p. clxxxviii *n*.

horrid dog in a kennel in the church near pele altar in the nave. The precentor does not feed the vergers and bell-ringers. The choir boys have no fuel allowed them in winter; their charcoal (probably for thuribles) is brought late, nothing is provided for their breakfasts but bread, the customary sweetened hasty pudding (a mess of flour, honey and milk[1]) for Friday and Saturday is withholden.

In the next place (7 June 1438) ten Residentiary Canons (viz. Precentor, Chancellor, Treasurer, three Archdeacons, Subdean, and three others) presented as many as forty-two articles, and seven other complaints, against the Dean, in which most, if not all, of the old charges were included; and it was alleged (no. 10) that he tried (as we say) to get behind Bp Flemmyng's award (1421), that he contravened it (*passim*), that he disregarded (no. 32) the order of Bp Gray (1434), although he had taken an oath in the presence of the High Treasurer of England to observe it. The Canons craved also an authoritative interpretation of certain phrases found in Flemmyng's *Laudum* as well as of the older awards of Grosseteste (1245), J. de Dalderby (1314), and Beaufort (1404). Nine days later the Dean opened fire with a counter-charge consisting of fourteen articles. He charged the Canons with misappropriating the stock of cloth which was kept in the Cathedral for the benefit of the poor (art. 9)[2], with letting their lodgings in

[1] Cf. the 'Honey Sop' on Good Friday. W. T. Warren, *Hosp. of St Cross*, p. 62, 1899.

[2] Some of the accounts preserved at Lincoln contain a mention of this cloth. Thus in the *Computus* of Ric. Meelys, Clericus Commune et receptor generalis Lincoln., A.D. 1452—3, we find an account *pro distributione panni* under the head "*Custus cere et Aliorum dudum supportatorum de communis mortuorum: Debet* in vir^{te} duodeñ panni lanei, coloris molderusset empt. hoc anno (with other cloth, carriage, candles, wax, payment to vicars and 'cantantes organum' for the Lady Mass, *hora prima*, &c. &c.)...40*l*. 16*s*. 2¾*d*." In a later year (1458—9) he writes under the like head: "D^{t} in xx^{ti} duodenis panni leanẹi coloris musterdevillers viz. iiij^{or} duod. panni lati et xvj duod. panni stricti. viz. le streytes empt' apud Nunduñ de Stirbrigg, de Will'mo Gale ad diu's p'c, cum iiij^{s} solut' pro † empens' Rob^{ti} Hide dictum pannum ementis et equitantis a Linc' vsque Stirbrig. et in redeund &c. in toto. 14*l*. 14*s*. 4*d*." A mixed grey woollen cloth was made at Mustrevilliers in France.

the close fall to ruin by neglect of repairs (art. 14), refusing him access to their muniments (art. 11), with keeping chantry-chaplaincies vacant and abusing Cardinal Repyngdon's decree for the union of the lesser chantries[1] as a source of lucre (artt. 6, 7), and he laid against them other charges of a more general and less tangible character.

After carefully analysing Bp Alnwick's decisions upon these charges and counter-charges, I do not hesitate to say that he dealt faithfully with the task of arbitration laid upon him. So far from shewing any desire to humiliate the Dean, he not only paid attention to every one of the complaints or charges which Macworth brought against the Canons, in a series of thirteen articles to which he gave the place of honour in his award, but he also quietly passed over such personalities as the alleged irregularity of the Dean's walk in the procession, and even let pass the more serious matter of the building of Macworth's stables (mentioned in the Canons' complaint, nos. 11, 33), the former, I suppose, as unworthy of attention in a serious document, the other, it may be, as irremediable.

Other articles which the Canons alleged (nos. 6, 9, 12, 16, 18, 26, 28, 29, 35, 36, 37, 39, 40) he has not dealt with distinctively in his *Laudum*. Some of them he may have considered to have been, in principle, covered by such articles as nos. 18 and 25, 36, 33; others perhaps on enquiry were not proven against the Dean. No. 30, which answers to the 30th complaint of the Chapter, was given by the Bishop in the Dean's favour. Their 23rd and 39th complaints may have seemed to him unsuitable

The name was commonly corrupted into 'mustard devils' in England. (See *Paston Letters*, i. 83, ii. 119, ed. Ramsay; Rock's *Textile Fabrics*, p. 74.) Sturbridge Fair was held near Cambridge in September at Holy Cross tide till Michaelmas. It was established by grant of King John, cir. 1211, and only lost its importance at the end of the 18th century. See Prof. J. E. B. Mayor's edition of the *Life of Ambrose Bonwicke*, pp. 19, 153—165.

[1] A list of Lincoln Chantries affected is given *L. C. S.* III. pp. 439—441. We find a record of the union of small chantries at St Paul's in 1391. *Registrum Statutorum S. Pauli*, pp. 142, 145. An account of Lincoln Chantries is given in *L. C. S.* II. pp. ccli—cclxix.

for his decision, as they concerned the royal prerogative[1]. And in like manner their 29th charge trenched on the burning question of the papal jurisdiction in England. Some articles his award contained over and above the points directly raised by the parties in the litigation. Articles 39, 40 are simply necessary clauses to secure the valid execution of the *Laudum* itself. Nos. 14—18 (though very probably no secular judge might have felt at liberty to interpose them) are concerned with such matters as one who felt himself to be a 'Father in God,' and visitor of the Church, would introduce, 'in season, out of season,' to insure that the rights of the inferior ministers of the Church were not overlooked, and that the furniture and ornaments of Divine service were not neglected by a Treasurer who, as we learn from Dean Macworth's order in the *Black Book* (p. 401), required some supervision. Nos. 35, 37 deal with topics suggested by the Chapter in their general conclusion (p. 68).

It speaks well for Bp Alnwick's integrity that the award which he delivered 23 June 1439, was received by both parties[2]; and, from that day to this, every Dean, dignitary, and Canon has expressly sworn or declared his hearty acceptance of it on the occasion of his installation.

Looking at the history of the feud between Dean Macworth and the Canons with the experience of the event before us, we may find it easy now to express a wish that W. Alnwick had paused here, and had been content to leave well alone, after achieving so desirable a consummation. But to him the whole seemed better than the half. He saw what he justly considered a defect

[1] The Bishop's 34th article may, however, have been called forth by the 39th complaint of the Chapter.

[2] It appears from the Rolls of Parliament, v. 10 (cited by Archd. G. G. Perry, *Lincoln Dio. Magazine*, vii. p. 84), that Alnwick's *Laudum* was fortified by an Act of Parliament (Session held on the morrow of St Martin, 1439), but the parties expressed their satisfaction for the time being in a practical manner by giving a promise to receive such newly codified statutes as the Bishop should compile.

in the Lincoln constitution, and he made a determined attempt to apply a remedy somewhat prematurely, with a result which for the time at least was most disastrous.

It is possible, as the late Dean of Lincoln (the Very Rev. J. W. Blakesley) once suggested, that there was a serious difference of opinion between the then Bishop and the Dean in matters political, as well as in their personal characters. Dr Macworth, who had been Chancellor to 'Prince Hal,' may have belonged to the party of which Humphry Duke of Gloucester was the head, while it is certain that Bp Alnwick (like his successor Marmaduke Lumley) belonged to the other side, which included Card. Beaufort and the Earl of Suffolk. Soon after he had delivered his award at Lincoln, Alnwick was associated with them and with others in conducting the trial of Eleanor Cobham for witchcraft, in 1441. Unhappily this brought him into partnership with two of the most unpopular men in England, W. Ascough (Bp of Salisbury) and Adam Moleyns (Dean of Salisbury, and in 1445 Bp of Chichester), both of whom were subsequently murdered by the mob in 1450. They had (says the English Chronicle) a character for covetousness and wickedness; and, though this fault certainly did not belong to the Bishop of Lincoln, it might tend to make him unpopular that he had been in any way connected with birds of that feather. It was however over the politics of his own Chapter, and in the service of an excellent cause, the cause of peace and justice, that Alnwick met with his reverse.

He knew that the Dean and Chapter had been at issue among themselves for several generations; there were sundry burning questions, and the customs and statutes of the Church to all appearance had supplied much of the fuel for the flames. What remedy could be found so effectual as to reduce the customs and statutes of Lincoln to an intelligible code? The Dean and the Canons with one voice allowed that such a book was what is sometimes styled a felt need, and the Bishop was qualified to supply it.

Bp Alnwick's royal master visited Winchester College July 30th, 1440, with a view to studying the statutes which William of Wykeham had drawn up in 1400. These he transcribed for the basis of his own codes for King's College and Eton, which were published in 1443 and 1444 respectively. In Sept. 1440 Alnwick, as Bp of the great and extensive diocese in which Eton at that time was situated, having been admitted into the king's confidence, appointed Lyndewood the canonist, and T. Bekynton (both of them Lincoln Canons probably), Ri. Andrew, first Warden of All Souls, and Bp Ayscough as his commissaries to carry out the conversion of Eton parish church into a collegiate church; and in that church Alnwick assisted at the consecration of Bekynton to the see of Bath and Wells, 13 Nov. 1443[1]. A month later he was one of the witnesses who attested King Henry's confirmation of the Liberties of St Paul's Cathedral at Westminster. That Alnwick's judgment and impartiality were well established may be further concluded from the fact that in 1448 he was called in to mediate between the Abbat of Croyland and Lord Dacre, and that he delivered his award in their case in that year. It is dated 21 Sept. 1448 and is written in the vulgar tongue[2].

While Henry VI. was preparing for his visit to Winchester, his confessor had issued notice of his intention to hold a Visitation of all the prebends and prebendal churches in the diocese of Lincoln[3]. Dean Macworth, although he had (nominally at least) accepted the *Laudum* of the preceding year, looked upon this intended exercise of the Bishop's undoubted right as a declaration of war against the privileges and liberties of the Chapter. He at once took steps to thwart the Bishop's design by issuing (24 June 1440) an urgent summons to all the prebendaries to confer with him at Lincoln in the Chapter-House on Thursday, 22 September, a week before it should

1 See Bekyngton's Letters, ed. Williams.

2 10 Dec. 1443. See Sparrow Simpson's *Registrum*.

3 Dugdale, *Monast.* ii. p. 122.

be too late to shew to the Bishop any ground of exemption which any of them might be able to allege[1]. In the meanwhile he was procuring from the Dean and Chapter of Salisbury (25 Aug. 1440) a statement of their privileges extracted from the Osmund Register, the Statute of Giles de Bridport (1262) &c. to the effect that Canons of Sarum were not required to answer the Bishop's examinations anywhere save in the Chapter-House, and that their prebends in general were exempt from episcopal visitation[2]. Canons of Sarum had their court in their prebends, with ordinary jurisdiction there and archidiaconal dignity therein, and the Dean of Sarum was visitor in the prebends. The Bishop of Salisbury had, in this matter, jurisdiction only in his own prebend (of Pottern), and the right of admitting and instituting Vicars in the prebendal churches upon episcopal manors[3].

Now at Lincoln, as I have said already, the relation of the Bishop to the Chapter was not identical with that at Salisbury[4]. There was indeed in the *Black Book* a similar

[1] *Black Book*, p. 402. [2] *Ibid.* pp. 404—5.

[3] I am gratified to find in the newly-recovered documents that Bp Alnwick anticipated me in this observation, *Lincoln Cathedral Statutes*, III. p. 445. 'Prebende Lincoln et prebende Sarum non sunt eiusdem nature.' See his remarks in that context.

[4] See *Lincoln Cathedral Statutes*, II. p. cli. An interesting extract from the *Lichfield* 'Liber Niger,' fo. 184, is cited by Mr Reynolds, who, unfortunately, does not give the date. *Wells Cathedral*, p. clxi. It shews the differences observed between seven cathedrals of the 'old foundation.'—'Apud Herford, pendet causa inter Episcopum Decanum et Capitulum super premissa.' For Lincoln, the writer refers to the definitive sentence given by Innocent IV. to Grosseteste. At Chichester, apparently, the Bishop could only order the roof to be mended and such like ordinary matters.

At St Paul's, London, the Bishop can only visit 'vacante decanatu.' At Wells the Dean is the only visitor of the Chapter. At Sarum he visits the Dean, and the city of Salisbury, but not the Chapter.

The tradition at York was that the Dean was superior even to the Primate, in Chapter. 'Dicunt quod [Decanus] in ecclesia maior est post archiepiscopum, et in Capitulo maior omnibus,' p. 93, below.

At Salisbury (as it is observed by Canon Jones, *Fasti*, p. 206) even Roger De Mortival, who had been Dean of Lincoln, and a stickler for his real or supposed rights of jurisdiction, when he became Bishop of Sarum,

exemption of Lincoln Dean and Canons from answering the Bishop elsewhere than in the Chapter, but the case of an appeal to Pope or Bishop was contemplated[1]. Moreover the *Liber Niger* at Lincoln did not, like the Sarum Custom Book, begin with a description of the Dean's dignity, but of the Bishop's; and this is in fact the keynote of the whole. This appears to us the more remarkable when we bear in mind that whereas the old register at Salisbury was the work of a bishop, the *Black Book* at Lincoln was compiled not in the interests of a bishop but of the Chapter. It contains moreover a copy of the bull which Grosseteste procured in 1245, in which, while the duty of punishing delinquents is maintained for the Dean, and only passes out of his hands to the Bishop in case of

voted in Chapter there *by proxy* at the vote on reception of his own Statutes in 1319. ('Nobis Rogero, prebendario de Poterne' heads the second class of votes, *Sarum Statutes*, p. 26.) Again in the 'Pentecostal Chapters,' the gatherings of the larger Chapter which were held there cir. 1560—1740 (as well as more recently), the Dean of Salisbury always took the Chair, even though the Bishop might be present. *Fasti*, p. 219. Such may be the case in some Chapter-Houses. But in the 'Church' the Bishop, or Archbishop, is alway *Ordinarius*. He is called so at Lincoln in Alnwick's *Laudum*, which Dean Macworth accepted:—see below. Compare the observations in the *Quarterly Review*, vol. cxxx. no. 259, pp. 239—240, and Chancellor F. C. Massingberd's Essay on *Cathedral Reform* in Howson's *Cathedral*, p. 180. See also the printed Opinion of Sir Ro. Phillimore and Dr Tristram (Doctors' Commons, Dec. 9, 1864), who determine that the Bishop is as much the Ordinary of his own Cathedral Church as he is in any church in the diocese. These authorities were noted in Bp Wordsworth's *Twelve Addresses*, p. 31.

"The Bishop of a diocese is called a 'Father in God,' and the Cathedral Church is called the 'Mother Church of the diocese.' 'It is,' says Gibson (*Codex*, tit. viii. cap. 1, p. 171), 'the parish church of all in the diocese. [See *Skinner*, p. 101.]'" *Twelve Addresses*, p. 29. *Theophilus Anglicanus*, part i. cap. 15 and note.

'Our cathedrals are the standard and rule to all parochial churches of the solemnity and decent manner of reading the liturgy, and administering the holy sacraments,' writes Abp Sheldon to the residentiary canons throughout his province 4 June 1670. Cardwell, *Doc. Annals*, 2nd ed. vol. ii. p. 331. Compare Q. Elizabeth's *Letter* to Abp Parker, 22 Jan. 1560—1, and the *Order in Council* for St Gregory's Church, 3 Nov. 1633. *Ibid.* i. 297; ii. 238. Dennis Granville, 1665. Surtees Soc. *Miscell.* xxxvii. p. 143.

[1] Lincoln *Black Book*, p. 283.

the Dean's negligence, the Bishop's jurisdiction is asserted as that of Visitor not of the Cathedral Church and Chapter alone, but over 'all prebendal churches, and churches of the dignities and of the Communa' and 'of the vicars, chaplains, and parishioners belonging to the said churches[1].' It does not appear that Bp Alnwick denied that the Dean himself was bound also to visit the prebends triennially or to receive reasonable procuration fees (which the Bishop himself did not take from the Chapter)[2]. He merely was maintaining his own right as Bp of Lincoln to hold episcopal Visitations upon the prebends in his diocese.

There was a letter of Robert de Chesney, Bp of Lincoln cir. 1160 (Gilbert de Sempringham being one of the witnesses), remitting to the prebends of Lincoln all rights and claims, exempting the churches of the prebends and of the Canons' community from archidiaconal fees or exactions, and from power to implead their 'men,' and adding the important clause 'sed eandem omnino habeant Canonici libertatem in prebendis suis quam habent Canonici Salesbiriensis ecclesie in suis[3].'

This privilege ought certainly to have been pleaded against Bp Grosseteste by the Canons in 1245. But, if it were, Pope Innocent IV. gave to it an interpretation fatal to such a contention as Dean Macworth put forward against the Bishop two centuries afterwards. But there was another matter, beside the Visitation of his prebend of Nassington, which caused the Dean misgivings. Along with the Canons he had given his consent to a proposal which the Bishop had made in the previous year (June

[1] *Black Book*, pp. 316, 318.

[2] *Novum Registrum, Lincoln Cathedral Statutes*, II. p. 277, *marg.*; cf. p. 447.

[3] *Black Book*, pp. 309, 310. St Hugh (cir. 1191—5) confirmed this charter of Bp Robert, exempting the prebendal churches from the power of the archdeacon, and extended the same to three other churches; 'Seuerebi, que ad luminaria Linc' ecclesie est assignata, et ecclesia de Lehton, que est de subdecanatu Lincoln, et ecclesia Omnium Sanctorum in Linc', que pertinet ad cancellariam.' (D. ii. 55, box 2.) Walter de Coutances (cir. 1183—5) had given a monition to archdeacons and their officials to respect the rights of the canons. (D. ii. 60, box 2.)

1439), to submit for the consideration and approval of the Chapter a *New Register*, or Draft Code of customs and statutes, *of the Church of Lincoln*, and this was to be presented to them at the Visitation of the Cathedral Church and Chapter after Michaelmas.

ALNWICK'S 'NOVUM REGISTRUM.'

Bishop William Alnwick depended chiefly upon the Black Book for his ideas of the special customs of Lincoln, of which he had only some four years' experience; but as a skeleton, and something more than a setting for the whole work, he adopted, with very few omissions, the well-digested *Corpus Juris* of St Paul's Cathedral which Ralph de Baldok had drawn up when he was Dean in London (1294—1305), and which may be read in Dr Sparrow Simpson's *Registrum Statutorum Eccl. Cath. S. Pauli London.* Four of the five parts of a book drawn for Lincoln on such lines Bp Alnwick delivered to the Chapter Clerk, Friday 7 Oct. 1440 (p. 448), having read the sections concerning the Bishop, Dean, Precentor and Chancellor (the treasurer was absent) at the meeting on the previous Monday. The absolute perspicuity of a legal treatise in five books would in itself not necessarily commend its contents to a man of Macworth's calibre,—one who was not over fond of obeying rules,—and it would be distasteful to others who had grown up among the traditions of Lincoln where (to reverse the old Cambridge phrase)[1] each was ready and prepared if necessary to pledge himself, if not *veris, consueta*, at least *scriptis, non scripta antehabiturum.* When K. Henry VI. provided for his two rising colleges their new statutes, couched to a very great extent in the language conceived by William of Wykeham in (then) comparatively recent times (i.e.

[1] Cf. *Statuta Trin. Coll. Cant.*, the Oath or Declaration of Fellows and Scholars, capp. xii, xiii (pp. 29, 32; 4° *Cantab.* 1844).

while his royal predecessor was Prince of Wales), he was but as one who puts new wine into new bottles. But when Bp Alnwick sought to bind Dean Macworth to the precise London code of Ralph Baldok, amplifying it with certain passages out of the Lincoln Black Book, to which the Dean (though inclined to keep the original volume in his own custody) had not hitherto shewn himself very ready to pay obedience, and incorporating a plain digest of the brand-new Award, it was like trying to bind the wild locks of Samson in a neat but slender web.

Bradshaw has described for us the second draft of the *Novum Registrum*[1] which Matthew Parker carried off from Lincoln when he was deprived in Q. Mary's time, and which he bequeathed to Corpus Christi College Library at Cambridge. We have printed this draft (pp. 268—363) shewing how far it agrees with the London Statutes[2] and what amendments were proposed at the committee-meetings in Lincoln Chapter-House. These meetings were above forty in number, and extended over a period of three or four years. The meeting (*convocatio*) does not appear to have been entirely confined to the members of the Chapter; for the Bishop in his preamble says that, besides the Canons, dignitaries and other officers of the cathedral whom he summoned, there were present on June 9th, 1439, certain other 'discreet persons &c.' whom

[1] The *Black Book*, pp. 156—8.

[2] Bradshaw has added in the margin of the *Novum Registrum* those numerals which shew where portions of Alnwick's book were derived from the Statutes of St Paul's: e.g. in *Lincoln Cathedral Statutes*, III. on p. 273, '1. 2,' '1. 3' = pars 1, cap. 2, and pars 1, cap. 3 of the London Statutes.

Here and there he puts the small circle 'o,' shewing where the Lincoln draft *departed* from the London rules, e.g. p. 273, *margin*.

The chapters adopted by Bp Alnwick from the St Paul's Statutes (though not precisely in the same order) appear to be these.

All the five proems.

Part I. 1—3, 6—15, (18) 19—25, 27, 28, 32, 36, 37, 50—55, 57—62.

Part II. 1—8, 15, 23.

Part III. 1, 2, 11, 13, 15, 18—23, 25, 29, 30, 35.

Part IV. 1, 3—9, 13—18, 20, 21.

Part V. 2, 3, 5, 6, 19.

he associated with them for the purpose. (*Discretis viris &c. comparentibus, et in Capitulo adunatis,* is the phrase used.) The second meeting was immediately after Michaelmas 1440, when the book was submitted in its first draft. The book which we have before us shews the work in a later stage, with some of the amendments or additions inserted in the text and others inserted in the margin, apparently in the Bishop's own hand, and sometimes re-considered and disposed of as the discussion advanced. The meetings were continued through 1441, and certainly until the spring or summer of 1442[1]. On the 9th of April 1442 Dean Macworth protested formally against the *Novum Registrum,* in the Chapter-House, before the Bishop's commissary; and when Alnwick at the subsequent meeting (May 29th) came in person, and asked whether he would accept it, 'dixit venerabilis vir decanus quod nunquam preberet consensum eidem, nec ipsis nouis ordinacionibus quouismodo consentiret: immo pocius reclamaret, cum talia ordinaciones et statuta, vt asseruit, in graue preiudicium dignitatis sue per consensum ipsius redundarent.'

I cannot do better than introduce here the account of these transactions furnished to the Cathedral Establishment Commissioners by Dean Blakesley and the Chapter of Lincoln 1879.

"William Alnwick, who was consecrated Bishop of Lincolñ in the year 1436, and who succeeded by means of the arbitration [or *Laudum* of June 23rd, 1439] in bringing a long and complicated litigation between John Mackworth, then Dean of Lincoln, and his Chapter to a pacific conclusion, thereupon formed the design of compiling a digest of all existing decisions, expunging

[1] Not improbably they were still going on in the spring of 1443. See *Lincoln Cathedral Statutes*, III. p. 462, and *note* there. The term *Convocatio* (rather than *Capitulum*) seems to have been studiously applied to a '*generale* capitulum' (p. ciii) or large meeting of Canons summoned to Lincoln to meet the Bishop in the Chapter-House. It is used by Bp Gray in Sept. 1434, and by Bp Alnwick in 1440. See *L. C. S.* II. p. clxvi, III. pp. 269, 270; cf. pp. 443, 444, *marg.*, 447, 453, 501.

whatever was superfluous, and reconciling what was apparently contradictory, in the view of precluding, so far as might be, all future disputes.

"For this purpose he convened, apparently in the usual manner through the Dean and Chapter, all the Dignitaries of the Cathedral, and all the non-residentiary Canons, or Prebendaries, and propounded his design on June 9th†, 1440, just about a year after the promulgation of the *Laudum*[1]†.

"The project was received with approbation, and by the unanimous consent of the parties assembled the 'convocation' (as it is styled) was 'continued' to the first '*dies iuridicus*' succeeding the next following Michaelmas-day, for the purpose meanwhile of drafting the new code.

"It appears that the Bishop, or certain '*discreti uiri*' who undertook this task, believed that something more than a digest would be desirable, and thought proper to introduce some new provisions, which appeared to them or to the Bishop likely to be advantageous in the future.

"We have not been able to find [1885] any record† of what took place on the '*dies iuridicus*' immediately after Michaelmas 1440, to which the June 'convocation' was 'continued.' The acts of Chapter for some years before and after this time are very defective, but it would appear that, with whatever unanimity the original project may have been received, the introduction of new matter gave rise to much opposition, and finally brought about the formal rejection of the new code, so far as it altered the existing customary rights of the Dean.

"The refusal of that dignitary is set forth formally in

[1] The *year* '1440' is not mentioned in the *Novum Registrum* (*Lincoln Cathedral Statutes*, III. p. 269), and the inference which (like the late Dean) we have there, in the margin, drawn from the page which follows it, has been shewn to be incorrect by my discovering in the summer of 1894 the original record, which shews that Bp Alnwick had proposed, and the Dean and Chapter had accepted the principle of, his New Register, on the same occasion as that on which they undertook to abide by his Award, June 9, 1439.

two protests (which we append)[1]. They are made solemnly in the Chapter-House in the presence of notaries public and witnesses, whose names are given, the first one (on April 9th, 1442) before the Bishop's Commissary; the second (on May 29th, 1442) before the Bishop himself, who is recorded to have put the direct question to the Dean, whether he would accept the new book containing the new ordinances, and to have received from the Dean the direct answer that he altogether refused to do so. It is perhaps worth while to point out that from the terms of this latter record it may be inferred that no less than 36 meetings of the 'continued convocation' had taken place between the assemblage at Michaelmas 1440 and the decisive rejection of the 'new book' on April 9th, 1442 [by the Dean]. Of these we can find no record." (*Cath. Establ. Commission*, Lincoln, Appendix, p. (5), 1885.)[2]

I must leave it to the reader, who has both the *Liber Niger* and the *Novum Registrum* before him, to determine how far the Dean of Lincoln in 1442 was justified in his opinion that the terms proposed in the latter were prejudicial to that measure of dignity and independence which the early book, and custom under it, had secured to himself and to his predecessors.

[1] For Dean Macworth's protests, see *Lincoln Cathedral Statutes*, III. pp. 456—8.

[2] If the number present on the two occasions, 9 April and 29 May 1442, which have been mentioned in the text, be fairly representative of the majority of the forty adjourned meetings, it is pretty obvious that the Bishop and the *principales personae* had the discussion generally to themselves. Consequently the draft of the *Novum Registrum* (*L. C. S.* III. pp. 269 ff.) represents an attempted digest on which the most determined critics had done their worst. We may infer also, as the meetings were so numerous, that up to the point of the Dean's expressed dissent the work of the Committee had been carried on in earnest, and considerable progress must have been made. Saving the Dean's dissatisfaction as to his dignity, I am inclined to think that we have in the *Novum Registrum, with its* marginalia, a fair account of what the Chapter of the day recognised as their custom at Lincoln, down to the time when Bp Alnwick issued his Award in 1439, and inclusive of that declaration, although it may have been expressed too much in language learnt 'within the sound of Bow bells.'

It was Bishop Christopher Wordsworth's opinion (after examining the episcopal register of Alnwick) that the ground of Dean Macworth's opposition was in reality some detail of ceremonial, such as the manner in which the Dean was to be censed in choir. I am happy to be able now to quote the following extract from T. Gascoigne's *Loci e libro veritatis* (ed. Thorold Rogers, p. 153), not only because it shews the truth of the conjecture which my father made, but because it tells us how the Dean's conduct appeared to a contemporary:—

'Ut nuper ostensum est in materiis controversie episcopi Lincolniensis domini Willelmi Alnwyk, et partis sibi aduerse decani superbi eiusdem ecclesie, qui optauit ut tociens sibi turificaretur, sicut episcopo; et, si episcopus esset presens in ecclesia Lincoln, quod nec episcopus, nec alius, inciperet officium in ecclesia illa, quousque decanus stallum suum intrauit: ex qua controuersia plurima mala secuta sunt.'

Bp Alnwick's register, although unfortunately it was not very regularly kept, shews plainly enough that, however mortified the Bishop may have been at the Dean's rejection of his digest or *corpus juris*, he accepted his defeat in the spirit of a constitutional ruler; and we hear no more of his *Registrum* being held to be in full force until 230 years after his decease.

Whether Macworth subsequently threw to the winds his solemn promise made in 1439, as he appears to have disregarded the similar obligation of 1421, and the less formal sentence which Bp Gray issued in 1434, and the agreement made with his Chapter at Sleaford in 1436, or whether his offences took some other direction, the records do not shew. It is clear however that Bp Alnwick found cause to take proceedings 22nd March 1443, and to require the Dean to answer personally to charges brought against him at the Visitation (18 April 1443); then to inhibit him; then to cite him (18 May 1444) to give account for having presumed to act while under sentence of inhibition; and lastly to pronounce sentence of excommunication

against him (10 Feb.), and to issue a commission (25 Mar. 1447) to proceed[1] against him as contumacious, for failing to appear at the Visitation. Whether the breach between the Dean and the Bishop was healed before the death of the latter in Dec. 1449, or not, I have no positive evidence to shew. W. Alnwick was buried in the western part of the Cathedral Church, in the place where he used to stand at the processions[2]. Dean Macworth lived just two years longer, and founded a chantry between the two easternmost pillars of the south aisle of the nave, and (as Mr Maddison told me) the chantry altar was that of St George. The Treasurer's inventory in 1536 and the Dean's in 1548 shew that there remained in the vestry at Lincoln for nearly a century a chasuble of white damask with flowers of gold, two tunicles and three albes with the apparell, having in the back an image of our Lady with her Child, of the gift of Mr J. Macworth, dean of Lincoln. Item thirteen copes of the same suit, with orphreys of blue velvet figured with flowers of gold, with two tunicles,

[1] *Bp Alnwick's Register*, fo. 51, 44, 56, 73. At the Bishop's primary visitation in 1437, W. Derby, Archd. of Bedford, had declared that on the vigil of St Peter and St Paul, 28 June, 1435, at evensong Dean Macworth had entered the choir with an armed body of men, had assaulted P. Partrich, the Chancellor, dragging him downward on to a bench by his almuce, and otherwise maltreating him. An independent account of this affray has quite recently been brought to light. In the records of the City Corporation of Lincoln (Reg. i. fo. 6^b) is an extract from the Plea-rolls of a trial at Westminster in Hilary term 1436, involving the question of civil jurisdiction. It appears that eight of Dean 'Makeworthe's' servants (including, I regret to say, our friend T. Atkyn notary, T. Cokayne chaplain, Nic. Bradbourne gent.) and sundry grooms and others, in warlike array, set upon Chancellor Partrych, while he was in his stall at evensong on 28th June, 1435, and went about to kill him, as it was thought, dragged him out of his stall, and tore his habit all to pieces. The indictment was quashed on technical grounds. (See kalendar by W. D. Macray, *Record Commission, Report*, XIV. (1895), Appendix viii. p. 21.)

[2] It is a subject for regret that the series of circular Processional Stones which remained in the pavement down each side of the nave at Lincoln until 1782 were then removed, and thus all trace of the formation of the mediæval procession was obliterated. Bishop Alnwick's position was by the third pillar from the west end, on the north side.

also of his gift[1]. These may have been an ordinary bequest, as were (no doubt) the great silver-gilt rood, with T. Beaufort's arms, and the costly cope of blue velvet which Bp Alnwick left to the cathedral church: but it will be remembered that Bp Gray had condemned the Dean to pay a fine to the cope fund, to the amount which he had neglected for many years to contribute for providing the *missa matutinalis*, also £87. 2*s.* 2*d.* to provide copes of the suit called 'the leopards' (such as Katharine Duchess of Lancaster had given previously) besides other vestments and ornaments, as well as choir copes to the value of £44, as fines for neglecting to pay septisms and vicar-stalls for twenty-two years. (See *L. C. S.* III. pp. 261—4[2].)

Leaving out of consideration his opposition to the proposed code of statutes, in which his action may by some be considered constitutional, there can be no reasonable doubt that John Macworth had set an example of disregard to the time-honoured statutes and ordinances of the church where he was Dean. The Precentor, Robert Burton, the next in command, who on several occasions had been one of the Dean's accusers, although not the most forward among them, now followed his example. In the spring of 1443—4 he is twice cited for contempt. He is called upon to make good the buildings of his house in the close which he has allowed to fall into a shamefully ruinous condition. In Jan. 1444—5 there is a charge against him for having violently attacked an acolyte, who approached to cense him at evensong on New Year's Day, and he snatched the censer out of his hand 'in an angry temper, like a madman.' Next day, when an officer came to affix the Bishop's mandate (probably upon the Precentor's stall) in the choir, Burton rated and abused him[3].

[1] See *Lincoln Inventories*, pp. 28, 53, in *Archæologia*, vol. 53 (1892).

[2] The composition fee for a choir cope at York in 1325 was 20 marcs (13*l.* 6*s.* 8*d.*) or twice the value of a palfrey (*L. C. S.* II. p. 129).

[3] 'vocando illum *scurram* et *vilem garcionem.*' The term *gartio* was commonly applied to camp-followers, oftentimes *mauvais garçons* as Ducange says, and many of the examples cited by him imply a connotation of contempt or discredit.

The day after, the Bishop issued a commission to Dr Tylney, keeper of St Peter's altar, and *auditor causarum*, to enquire into the Precentor's behaviour. He was served with sentence of inhibition, and then did his best to force the chaplains to desist from saying their masses during the term while he himself remained under sentence.

It is sufficiently evident that there were heart-burnings among the dignitaries at Lincoln as to the manner of censing the Dean, the Rulers of the Choir, and the Canons. The old statutes were indefinite in their directions[1], and it is evident that there was some discussion at the statute-revision committee-meetings in 1440—2 as to the part to be taken by the Bishop himself (p. 275), when two lines, not found in the St Paul's statutes, were introduced; the Precentor[2] claimed to have the management of the thurifers (a point not noticed in the Bishop's earlier draft of his *registrum*. See *L. C. S.* III. p. 299), and a note was made to the effect that the *stalla capitalia* (by which I suppose are meant the terminal stalls occupied by dean, precentor, chancellor, and treasurer) were to be censed (not from the step, but) from the floor of the church. On May 20th, 1443, the Canons assured the Bishop that they approved his Order for Censing, and would keep it. On May 1st, 1444, the Bishop issued an order to observe the rules for censing the choir. On the 9th the Chapter received the order and agreed to it. On the 22nd when the Subdean and four other canons, the Vice-chancellor

At Lincoln the word occurs occasionally in accounts of fees or small payments. See also *Lincoln Cathedral Statutes*, III. p. 466. Thus in the succentor's book of 1527 (lf. 23) among the subordinate ministers in receipt of an allowance under the head of wines, the last named, after the choristers, are 'laico sacriste, j. d.; gartioni eius, j. d.; sutori, siue sissori, iiij. d. (for attending to the linen), Lotrici, iij. d.' Two persons who assisted the vergers at St Paul's Cathedral, and were employed in bell-ringing, organ-blowing, sweeping, or menial offices, were called *garciones*. (*Registrum Statutorum*, pp. xlii, 109, 124, 225.)

[1] *Black Book*, pp. 273—4, 367—9, 372, 375, 379, 380.

[2] Precentor Burton and Peter Partrich, the Chancellor of the Cathedral, were among the seven representatives sent from England to the Council of Basel in 1431. They spoke boldly in defence of our national rights.

and four others, were assembled in Chapter, John Depyng, prebendary of Buckden, brought in the Bishop's 'statutes and ordinances' on the manner of censing the choir. The Subdean read them, and in the name of the Chapter promised to observe them. After business was concluded, in came Precentor Burton, and saw the order; but of course he was too late to alter the act of the Chapter; and, as we have observed, he vented his spleen upon the unoffending thurifer the first day of the following year. Burton died, or was removed, before the autumn of 1446.

The Bishop's statute *de modo incensandi*, which appears to have been quite legal and regular in form, and in its acceptance by the Chapter, is printed elsewhere[1]. It is difficult at this date to know in detail what the Precentor's grievance was[2]. He may have expected to be censed before the ruler of the choir on the *decani* side, or else to have had (like the Dean) the censer swung towards him four times, instead of only thrice like other canons. At Chichester the statutes of 1197 only prescribed 'quod singuli clerici in superiori gradu bis incensentur.' The regulations on this subject, as proposed while the *Novum Registrum* was under discussion at Lincoln, will be found on p. 299, lower margin[3].

The *Novum Registrum* was drawn up, like Ralph de Baldok's London Statutes, in five books or *particulae*, treating (1) of the Constitution, dignitaries and prebends of Lincoln, (2) the Canon's 'entrance' or installation,

[1] See *Lincoln Cathedral Statutes*, III. pp. 509—511. The Bishop (20 May 1443) asked the Canons at Lincoln, one by one, in Chapter, whether they would observe the Censing Statute which had been already issued (*editum*) with their consent. They answered severally that they approved it, and, Dean Macworth saying nothing to the contrary, the Bishop ordered it to be observed in future. But it soon became evident that he had been treading over hidden fires, 'suppositos cineri doloso.'

[2] In 1437 Ro. Burton represented to Bp Alnwick that the Chapter ought to have paid him the emoluments for the precentor's office for those four years in which he had been engaged at Basel on their behalf.

[3] *Liber Niger* &c., H. B.'s *Memorandum on the Books*, pp. 160, 161. *Alnwick's Register*, fo. 47, 45. See *Lincoln Cathedral Statutes*, III. pp. 512, 516.

(3) his 'progress' or residence, (4) his exit, by death or other cause, and (5) the chantry-priests, vicars, and inferior officers or servants of the church. It was perhaps not unnatural that the resistance opposed to the compilation related principally to the first book, which concerned the dignitaries. Selections from this had been read aloud at the meeting which was held on 7 Oct. 1440, and four books were delivered for inspection.

At all events we find that about five-and-twenty years after the deaths of Alnwick and Macworth, and thirty years after the departure of Precentor Robert Burton, in other words cir. 1475, in the days of Bp Rotherham and Dean Robert Fleming (nephew of Bp Richard Fleming), a *succès d'estime* was accorded to Bp Alnwick's efforts. The greater part of his *Novum Registrum*, that is to say the portion which consisted of books 2 to 5, was transcribed under the title of *Constitutiones Ecclesie Lincolñ super Laudum Dñi W. Alnwyk Lincolniensis Episcopi.* And somewhat later, about the year 1500, J. de Grantham, prebendary of Lyddington, transcribed these select 'Constitutions' again.

The substantial value of Bp Alnwick's compilation, as a convenient and perspicuous collection of customs, had begun to be recognised at last.

Further, a transcript of the entire *Novum Registrum* (all *five* books) was made in 1523, in the days of Bp Longland, when J. Constable was Dean. Another was copied (also in Longland's episcopate) in 1540; and about the same time, or a few years later, the Chapter Clerk, W. Snawdun, transcribed it once again. Moreover when Parker was Dean (in the time of K. Edward VI.) he studied the book so far as to make cross-references between the original volume (which he finally left to the Corpus Library) and a copy of the *Liber Niger* which is still at Lincoln (A. 2. 6). And other copies were made in later generations.

It must be admitted that this intended *Corpus Juris* never received a formal acceptance from the Dean and

Chapter, although the Canons at least, with more or less reluctance, consented to discuss it in detail[1], but this fact came to be overlooked or disregarded. The confused and somewhat vague *Liber Niger* fell at length out of consideration, and Alnwick's collection, once so indignantly rejected, survived as, in some sense, the fittest; and by that strange concurrence of events and causes, which Henry Bradshaw has so delightfully elucidated[2], the Dean and Chapter of one or two generations back, and their predecessors for two centuries or more, had come to *require* of all prebendaries on admission, and among these, of some of Alnwick's and Macworth's successors (whenever, that is, the Bishop or the Dean[3] claimed installation to a prebend) an oath or declaration of their determination to 'observe and keep' the very collection of Statutes which had been indignantly rejected in 1442. Consequently, when Bishop Wordsworth desired to print the Statutes of his cathedral in 1872—3, and (not having access to the Chapter muniments as a matter of right as Bishop) applied to certain of the Residentiary Canons for information and assistance in his undertaking, they assisted him in editing at his cost, and with a Latin introduction from his pen, the *Novum Registrum* of Alnwick, together with his *Laudum* (and the 'Statuta Vicariorum,' which proves to be

[1] Several of the records of the discussion are printed for the first time in the *Lincoln Cathedral Statutes* (Camb. 1897), having been, until recently, rendered quite illegible; and their contents were unknown when Henry Bradshaw visited Lincoln, and indeed were not suspected until they came into Canon Chr. Wordsworth's hands when a friend sent him the book that he might see another part of its contents which was written with darker ink. A word or two which he could read there excited his curiosity, and the application of ammonium sulphide revealed an account of the first reading of Alnwick's *Registrum*!

[2] The *Black Book*, 4—9, 217—222.

[3] The Dean, in the late 17th—19th centuries, did not *as Dean* swear to observe the *Novum Registrum* (nor had Alnwick himself required it), but only the *Laudum* and other customs. But whenever the Dean, or any other dignitary came to be installed into a prebend, they specified also 'all the Statutes, Customs and Ordinances, contained in the New Registry'—for so *Novum Registrum* came to be Englished in 1733.

a much earlier composition), from a copy which had been given to the Bishop by his predecessor as containing the Cathedral Statutes, and which had been made probably for Bishop J. Thomas in 1750, and extracted from the fuller volume of 1523, still in the possession of the Chapter. With his usual energy the Bishop made enquiries at Cambridge also. But an unfortunate blunder in Nasmith's catalogue concealed the real antiquity and true history of the MS. at Corpus Christi College, until six years after Dr Wordsworth's little collection of 'Statuta' was in print. Then a letter of further enquiry from him to Mr Lewis was passed on to Henry Bradshaw, with results which have been published in part in 1892, and partly in the second volume of the Statutes. Although, so far as we know, the book was never formally ratified or sealed, I thought it best in 1897 to include the *Novum Registrum* in the *Lincoln Cathedral Statutes*[1] partly because the Bishop's little book was printed privately, but more especially because the discovery of the *marginalia* in the draft at Cambridge (some of them possibly in Alnwick's own handwriting), with the appearance of the amendments attached to their proper context, places the text in a new light, puts an entirely new complexion upon many passages, and adds a fresh interest to the whole.

CHR. W.

NOTE ON THE WELLS CATHEDRAL COPY OF THE LINCOLN *NOVUM REGISTRUM* IN THE BOOK OF EVIDENCES OF W. COSYN, DEAN OF WELLS, 1498—1525.

In the summer of 1912 the Dean of Wells, Dr J. Armitage Robinson, kindly drew my attention to his discovery of a copy of the *Novum Registrum* of Bishop Alnwick of Lincoln being preserved among other documents

[1] The text of *Novum Registrum* (with its *marginalia* and amendments) is to be found in *Lincoln Cathedral Statutes*, III. pp. 268—363.

in a MS. book compiled in 1506 by William Cosyn, who held the deanery of Wells in 1498—1525. Early in Dr Cosyn's time, or indeed from 1498—1509, the Chapter at Wells were busy about their statutes. We know from the *Liber Ruber* that at Christmas, 1498, the book of Wells Statutes was to be corrected and bound and placed in the library for inspection. It was ordered in 1509 (1 Oct.) that the scattered statutes of Wells Cathedral should be collected by Mr Hugh Yng and Roger Church. Dean Cosyn had previously been Archdeacon of Bath for about a year before he succeeded John Gunthorp in the deanery of Wells, and apparently he held the prebend of *major pars altaris* at Salisbury in 1492—1505. As he held an archdeaconry in the diocese of Lincoln (Bedford) from 1494 to 1525, he was able to procure from Lincoln the document which his eminent successor has identified.

The volume at Wells, known as *Dean Cosyn's MS.*, is bound in rough calf and has the distinguishing mark 'E' upon the cover. It consists of paper and parchment mixed in such a manner as to suggest that in some instances at least the parchment leaves were inserted here among the paper simply for the sake of stiffening and strengthening the whole. At each end the binder has employed a waste page of an old French romance, Meliot de Logres, written on vellum in double columns.

The volume opens with—

p. 1. Antiqua statuta de officiis cuiuslibet persone ecclesie Cath[edralis] Wellen. (These statutes have been printed by the Rev. H. E. Reynolds in his *Wells Cathedral*, folio, 1881, pp. 55—68.)

p. 15. Prebends and Daily Psalter. (Reynolds, *u. s.* pp. 69—72.)

p. 16. Tabula installationum et taxacionis. (*Id.* pp. 97—99.)

p. 17. Forma collacionum cantariarum. (*Id.* p. 99.)

p. 18. Subsequens tabula describit eccia*m* (? eciam) annilarios videlicet presbiteros secular*um* (? seculares)

in ecclesia (∧ cathedrali) Welleñ, ad que altaria, et quantum quilibet percipiet, et sub qua forma debent conferri vel admitti, vt patet inferius. (*Id.* pp. 73, 74.)

pp. 19—29. Statutes of 'J. Goddele, nuper decani Wellen.' A.D. 1331. (*Id.* pp. 74—93; cf. p. 129.)

pp. 30, 31 are blank.

p. 32 (numbered as f. 16ᵇ). Taxacio. (Cf. Reynolds, p. 97.)

p. 33 = f. 17. In rotulis de particulis.

pp. 34—46 = ff. 17—23ᵇ. De ordinacione clericorum in choro...In introitu chori...iij. de excellencioribus. (*Id.* pp. 1—24.)

pp. 47, 48 = f. 24, blank.

pp. 49—122 = ff. 25—61ᵇ. Various evidences.

Quod decanus debet visitare capitulum et prebendas cum aliis ecclesiis.

[M]emorandum quod licet ad Reuerendos viros dños Decanum et Capitulum eccl. Cathedralis Well. pleno iure....

p. 120. Henricus Dei gracia Rex. Inspeximus. 25 Feb. a° 12°. s. sign. Fitzherbert.

Then references follow to passages 'In veteri Registro.' nota, pro graciis concessis ca° in f. 143°. nota, pro Jurisdiccione Decani, in f. 151°. nota, pro Sequestris fructuum in Chedson, in f. 152°, 154°, 155°.

p. 122. ...pro terris magistri Rodney apud Merkham, f. 123°.

f. 62 = pp. 123, 124, blank.

On p. 125 = f. 63, there are scribblings and pen-trials including lines from Horace (*Epist.* I. xviii, lines 68—71 not quite accurately remembered).

p. 126 is blank.

p. 127 = f. 64. [Novum Registrum Willelmi Alnewick Lincolniensis episcopi.] Begins '[U]niuersis et singulis...' ends p. 216 '...euagentur inhoneste.' It has no title here, the rubrication never having been added. Spaces are left here and there for the insertion of large capital initials, and occasionally for some missing word, which perchance the copyist was

unable to read in his exemplar in the sixteenth century.

On p. 215 the scribe has added a note at the foot of the last leaf but one of the document from Lincoln, apparently with some reference to the collation of chantries in the patronage of the Dean and Chapter:—"per nominacionem residenci[ar]iorum secundum primum eorum cursum si domino videatur (?) iuxta clausulam 'Ordinamus' positam in fine tercie partis parum ante rubricam 'De firmis assignandis.'" (The reference here is to the paragraph *Ordinamus eciam quod beneficia ad collacionem siue presentacionem communem Decani et capituli spectancia ad nominacionem singulorum residencium secundum cursum residencie per capitulum conferantur.* See *Statutes* (Bradshaw and Wordsworth), iii. 339 = *Novum Registrum et Laudum* (ed. 1873), p. 52.)

pp. 217–222, blank.

pp. 223–237 are vellum.

pp. 238–257, paper.

p. 223. [i]n nomine summe et indiuidue Trinitatis. Nos Thomas de Bekyntona...(first heading) De principali magistro choristarum.

pp. 245—257, blank.

On the last page (258) of the leaves of paper—among which occasional leaves of vellum are bound for stiffening the volume, as described above—there is this inscription :—

'liber Wilelmi Cosyn decani Wellen Ecclesie cathedralis.'

'Pertinet iste liber Willelmo Cosin Decano Wellen. scriptus et collatus labore et sumptibus suis anno domini ιησ (*in margin*, 1506).'

p. 258. De graciis concessis canonicis (7 lines). Nota pro iurisdiccione Decani Wellen.

pp. 258 to 360, with which the book concludes, all consist of vellum of various thicknesses.

The *Novum Registrum,* which reached Wells perhaps

by 3 June 1502, when Dr Cosin was installed in person (as in 1499 by proxy), and certainly not later than 1525 the year of his decease, is not the purely London Book of St Paul's, but it is the complete book of Bp Alnwick's compilation in 1440. It is, accordingly, something more than the Second Part only of the Draft *Novum Registrum* of which Henry Bradshaw has described the copy which, as he tells us, was written about 1475, and is still preserved among Lincoln Cathedral muniments (A. 2. Box 1. 7 §§§), and in which he recognised the exemplar of that portion of Bp Alnwick's work which is contained under the title of *Constituciones...super Laudum* in John Grantham's Book of 1500 (A. 2. 7).

Dean Cosyn's copy of the *Novum Registrum*, so far as I could judge when I was kindly invited to examine it at the Deanery in 1912, is closely allied to the complete copy which is contained in 'the Compilation of (about) 1523' made early in Bp Longland's episcopate, and now known at Lincoln as the *Chapter-Library Statute Book*, A. 427. I should not be surprised if a good judge of handwriting should recognise the script of the writer of one of the MSS. at Lincoln as being that of the clerk whose pen traced the copy of Bp Alnwick's book in Dean Cosyn's *Evidences* at Wells.

It belongs to the time at the very beginning of the 16th century, or the close of the 15th, when at Lincoln as well as at Wells an interest in the old Customs and Statutes was reviving; and when, as Bradshaw says, 'it seems to have been taken for granted, now, that Bp Alnwick's book contained actual *Constituciones ecclesie Lincolniensis.*' The *Black Book* (1892), p. 173.

CHR. W.

16 *January*, 1913.

The following Latin text is in the main that of Mr Bradshaw and Canon Chr. Wordsworth printed in *Lincoln Cathedral Statutes*, vol. III. pp. 187—228 (Cambridge: at the University Press, 1897).

Where it differs from the aforesaid text the corrections have been made from the contemporary MS. copy of the *Laudum* written by the notary Thomas Colston, which is still in the Muniment Room of Lincoln Cathedral.

* Lf. 1. *LAUDUM W: ALNEWIKE EPISCOPI LINCOLN. (A° 1439.)

WILL'MUS PERMISSIONE divina Lincolñ Episcopus dilectis filijs Capitulo ecclesie nostre cathedralis beate Marie lincolñ salutem, graciam et benediccionem.

In negocio compromissi super diuersis litibus et dissencionum materijs inter Magistrum Johannem Macworth decanum eiusdem ecclesie nostre ex parte vna, ac vos Capitulum predictum ex parte altera, suscitatis et exortis, in nos ut arbitrum, Arbitratorem, Laudatorem, sententiatorem, diffinitorem, &c[a], per dictum Magistrum Johannem Macworth decanum predictum et vos Capitulum predictum concorditer assumpt' hinc inde facti, cuius vtriusque videlicet submissionis siue compromissi tam per dictum Magistrum Johannem Macworth decanum predictum quam vos Capitulum predictum in nos facti tenor inferius describitur, rite procedentes; Laudum, Arbitrium, decretum, pronunciacionem, declaracionem, ordinacionem et diffinicionem nostram isto vicesimo tercio die mensis Junij Anno
(23° Jun. 1439.) Domini infrascripto in Domo Capitulari dicte Ecclesie nostre Lincoln ad hoc assignatis, dicto Magistro Johanne Macworth Decano predicto et vobis Capitulo predicto sufficienter coram nobis tunc comparentibus, in presencia Notarij et scribe nostri in hac parte, ac testium infrascriptorum, tulimus in hec verba :

THE AWARD OF WILLIAM ALNWIKE BISHOP OF LINCOLN

In the year 1439.

WILLIAM, by divine permission Bishop of Lincoln, to his beloved sons the Chapter of our Cathedral Church of Blessed Mary of Lincoln, salutation, grace and benediction.

In the matter of the composition on various differences and matters of disagreement which have been stirred up and have arisen between Mr John Macworth, Dean of our same Church, on the one side, and you the Chapter aforesaid on the other side, which has been by consent of both sides submitted, by agreement, to us as judge, arbitrator, awarder, adjudicator, definer, etc., by Mr John Macworth the Dean aforesaid, and by you the Chapter aforesaid, and of whose submission and consent to arbitration made to us on the part of both sides, alike by the said Mr John Macworth the Dean aforesaid as also by you the Chapter aforesaid, the contents are written out below; by due procedure we have put forth our award, judgement, decision, pronouncement, proclamation, ordinance, and definition, on this 23rd day of the month of June in the year of our Lord below written [viz. 1439] in the Chapter-House of our said Church of Lincoln, Mr John Macworth the Dean aforesaid, and you the Chapter aforesaid appearing then before us in sufficient representation being appointed to be present at the act, in the presence of our scribe and notary on our part and of the witnesses whose names appear below, in these words:

In Dei Nomine Amen. Dudum inter dilectos in Christo filios Magistrum Johannem Macworth Decanum Ecclesie nostre Lincolñ ex vna parte, et Capitulum eiusdem parte ex altera suggerente inimico humani generis pacis emulo post nonnullas consimiles licium occasiones per laudum bone memorie Ricardi episcopi tunc Lincoln predecessoris nostri sopitas, super diuersis articulis, materia discordie ac dissencionis, fuit denuo et est exorta: Tandem ijdem Decanus et Capitulum volentes huiusmodi iurgiorum radices abscindere, ne malis que ex litibus oriuntur aditum prebeant, in nos Wyllm̃ permissione diuina Lincoln Episcopum tanquam in arbitrum[1] Arbitratorem[2], &c[a], super reformanda pace et concordia inter ipsos Decanum et Capitulum ac super articulis huiusmodi omnibus et singulis, ac alijs per ipsos pendentibus, compromissis in nos factis tradendis de alto et basso absolute et libere compromittere curauerunt, prout in compromissorum Instrumentis publicis inde confectis plenius continetur quorum tenores seriatim sequuntur sub hac forma.

[1] *corr. from* -ium.
[2] *corr. from* -cionem.

(i.) Compromissum Capituli.

Reverendo in Christo Patri ac domino domino Wyllm̃o Dei gracia Lincolñ Episcopo vestri humiles filij et deuoti oratores Robertus Burton Precentor, Petrus Partrich Cancellarius, Johannes Haget Thesaurarius, Johannes Southam Archidiaconus Oxoñ, Wyllelmus Lassel Archidiaconus Huntyngdon, Wyllelmus Derby Archidiaconus Bedeford, Johannes Percy Subdecanus, Johannes Marshall, Ricardus Ingoldesby et Thomas Warde Canonici residenciarii Ecclesie vestre Lincoln Capitulum eiusdem facientes ob et ad inscripta capitulariter congregati, omnimode subjeccionis reverencie et honoris plenitudinem debitam tanto Patri.

[Decem canonici residentes. *P.*]

IN THE NAME OF GOD. AMEN. In as much as between our beloved sons in Christ MR JOHN MACWORTH Dean of our Church of Lincoln on the one side, and THE CHAPTER of the same on the other side, at the instigation of the enemy of the human race the hater of peace, after the settlement of divers like sources of strife by the award of Richard late Bishop of Lincoln of blessed memory, our predecessor, on various questions there has arisen afresh and has some time existed matter of dissension and disagreement; at length the same Dean and Chapter wishing to cut away the roots of such quarrellings lest they should afford ingress to the evils which arise from strifes, have undertaken definitely and of their own free will to submit to the settlement of us, William, by divine permission Bishop of Lincoln, as judge, arbitrator, etc. with a view to the restoration of peace and concord between themselves the Dean and Chapter and for the thorough and complete treatment of all and singular such articles and others depending on them, which have been submitted to our settlement, as is contained more fully in the public instruments made therefrom, and the general tenour of both of them being as hereinafter followeth in due order.

(i) THE 'COMPROMISE' OF THE CHAPTER.

The complaints of the Chapter against the Dean.

To the Reverend Father and Lord in Christ, the Lord William, by the grace of God Bishop of Lincoln, your humble sons and devoted bedesmen Robert Burton Precentor, Peter Partrich Chancellor, John Haget Treasurer, John Southam Archdeacon of Oxford, William Lassel Archdeacon of Huntingdon, William Derby Archdeacon of Bedford, John Percy Subdean, John Marshall, Richard Ingoldesby, and Thomas Warde, Canons Residentiary of your Church of Lincoln, representing the Chapter of the same, assembled in their capitular capacity on account of and in view of these written complaints, [render] in every way the fulness of submission, reverence and honour due to so great a Father.

Cum, iam pridem nonnullis litibus controuersijs et discordijs inter dudum Decanos dicte Ecclesie vestre
* Lf. 1b. residenciarios *qui pro tempore fuerunt, et presertim honorabilem virum Magistrum Johannem Macworth Decanum modernum ex parte vna ac Canonicos dicte Ecclesie residenciarios Capitulum eiusdem tunc facientes ex altera, in Romana curia et alibi in iudicio et extra iudicium sumptuosis quam plurimum agitatis, per laudum et arbitrium venerabilis patris Ricardi nuper Lincoln Episcopi predecessoris vestri, vigore compromissi in ipsum venerabilem patrem hinc inde facti, sopitis; Alie graves et scandolose inter predictum honorabilem virum Magistrum Johannem Macworth Decanum predictum modernum et nos Capitulum predictum illo procurante qui a principio ruine sue vnitatem ecclesie rescindere, et caritatem vulnerare invidie sue felle indies conatur denuo suscitentur questiones,

(Bp Fleming's Award, dated 27 May, 1421.)

De et super eo,

Questiones litis per Capitulum

[1.] Quod dictus Decanus iuxta laudabilem consuetudinem Ecclesie absente Episcopo non pascit chorum, siue ministros chori, in festis principalibus, quibus presens, absente Episcopo, et celebrare et pascere, absensque sic pascere tenetur.

[2.] Quodque dictus Decanus non obseruat onera sibi incumbencia in principalibus et alijs festis, Regumque et Episcoporum obitibus, iuxta quod intabulatur et intitulatur.

[3.] Insuper idem Magister Johannes Decanus dudum de Hempyngham et nunc de Nassyngton prebendarius et canonicus non residenciarius, toto tempore non residencie sue subtraxit vicarium suum, quem in choro dicte ecclesie suis sumptibus ad supportandum onera ipsius non

Since, although some time ago divers strifes, quarrels and differences between the former Deans residentiary of your said Church who then were, and in particular the worshipful Mr John Macworth the present Dean on the one side, and the Canons Residentiary of the said Church then forming the Chapter of the same on the other side, pursued in the Roman Curia and elsewhere in court and out of court at very great expense, were allayed by the award and judgement of the venerable Father Richard[1], late Bishop of Lincoln, your predecessor, in virtue of the composition made by both parties to that venerable Father: other serious and scandalous issues have again arisen between the aforesaid worshipful Mr John Macworth the present Dean aforesaid, and us the Chapter aforesaid (by the machinations of him who from the beginning of his own fall strives day by day to rend the unity of the Church and to wound charity by the gall of his own envy) concerning and over the following:

[The Complaints of the Chapter against the Dean.]

[1.] Because the said Dean does not according to the praiseworthy custom of the Church feed the choir or the ministers of the choir in the Bishop's absence on the principal Feasts, on which if he is present and the Bishop absent he is bound to officiate and feed, and if away so to feed.

[2.] And because the said Dean does not fulfil the obligations incumbent on him on principal and other Feasts, and at the obits of Kings and Bishops, according as he is scheduled and required to do.

[3.] Moreover the same Mr John the Dean, Prebendary lately of Empingham and at present of Nassington and Canon non-residentiary, during the whole time of his non-residence has withdrawn his vicar whom he is bound by the statutes and custom of the Church aforesaid to

[1] Bishop Richard Fleming's award was dated 27 May 1421.

residentis exhibere tenetur de statut' et consuetudine ecclesie antedicte.

[4.] Idem eciam Magister Johannes Decanus prebendarius et canonicus non residenciarius predictus toto tempore non residencie sue predicte subtraxit Canonicis residenciarijs septimas, quas racione dictarum prebendarum suarum ad communam canonicorum residenciariorum de eisdem statutis et consuetudinibus solvere tenetur.

[5.] Item quod idem Decanus detecta in visitacionibus Episcoporum per se solum contra consuetudines Ecclesie, absque communione Capituli, corrigere vsurpavit.

[6.] Item cum soli canonici residenciarij pascentes et celebrantes de consuetudine ecclesie percipiant et percipere debeant septimas solutas per non residenciarios in communam residenciariorum, dictus Decanus vendicat et exigit participacionem septimarum huiusmodi contra consuetudinem predictam.

[7.] Idem eciam Decanus moniciones et mandata alia que autoritate et nomine Decani et Capituli de statutis et consuetudine predictis fieri deberent et procedere: solo suo nomine et auctoritate decanali facit et emittit.

[8.] Idem eciam Decanus clericum suum suspectum ad actus capitulares inducit, contra formam laudi predicti, per quem secreta capitularia deteguntur.

[9.] Idem insuper Decanus medietatem correccionum canonicorum tam in visitacione sua decanali quam extra, detectorum, detinet a Capitulo; contra formam laudi predicti.

[10.] Quodque idem Decanus contra mentem et formam

maintain at his own charges for the performance of his duties when not in residence.

[4.] Also the said Mr John the Dean, Prebendary and Canon non-residentiary aforesaid, during the whole time of his non-residence aforesaid, has withheld the septisms[1] from the Canons Residentiary, which he is bound by the same statutes and customs to pay in virtue of his said prebends to the common fund of the Canons Residentiary.

[5.] Also because the same Dean has taken upon himself without consulting the Chapter, contrary to the customs of the Church, to correct by his sole authority things found wrong at episcopal Visitations.

[6.] Also, though only the Canons Residentiary who feed[2] and officiate, by the custom of the Church receive and should receive the septisms paid by the non-residentiaries to the common fund of the Residentiaries, the said Dean claims and exacts a share in these septisms contrary to the aforesaid custom.

[7.] Also the same Dean in his own name only and by his authority as Dean, makes and sends forth monitions and other mandates which by the statutes and custom aforesaid should be made and should proceed by the authority and in the name of the Dean and Chapter.

[8.] Also the same Dean brings his own clerk, whom we mistrust, to be present at the doings of the Chapter, contrary to the form of the aforesaid award, and by him the secrets of the Chapter are made public.

[9.] Moreover the same Dean holds back from the Chapter a half of the Canons' fines for things found wrong both in his own decanal visitation and outside it; contrary to the form of the aforesaid award.

[10.] Also because the same Dean contrary to the intention

[1] The 'septisms' payable by non-residentiaries were a yearly charge of one-seventh on the rateable value of each prebend. A few were exempted from payment, viz. c. solidorum, lx. solidorum, Thorngate, Bedford minor, St Botolph's and All Saints.

[2] 'feedings' (*pastus chori*) were provided on certain appointed days by the Canon of the week for ten officials (such as the sacrist, succentor, clerk of the works, etc.) at his table.

laudi predicti, exegit obedienciam a quibusdam Canonicis ante dictum laudum installatis.

[11.] Quod* eciam idem Decanus ('contra mentem' *struck out*) in processionibus non incedit directe et linealiter in ordine ex parte sua chori, iuxta consuetudinem Ecclesie, sed oblique et indirecte, aliquando post executorem officij, aliquando iuxta eum, contra consuetudinem huiusmodi.

* Lf. 2[a]. [Parker's numbering is wrong from this point onward.]

[12.] Quodque idem Decanus subtrait, et adiu subtraxit, quendam capellanum, quem suis sumptibus exibere et invenire tenetur, ad quotidie celebrandum missam matutinalem in dicta Ecclesia.

[13.] De eo quod idem Decanus non cohibet servientes suos impedientes ianitorem clausi quominus valeat portas clausi debito tempore claudere vt deberet.

[14.] Quodque idem Decanus adimit a Capitulo iurisdiccionem eidem Capitulo in prebendis, et earum prebendarijs, eciam post eorum mortem, extra visitacionem ipsius Decani in ejus absencia seu negligencia pertinentem et spectantem.

[15.] De eo eciam quod idem Decanus subtrahit a Capitulo ·xxvj· s· ·viij· d· quos soluere tenetur annuatim ad obitum Henrici Lexyngton in dicta ecclesia celebratum.

[16.] Quodque eciam idem Decanus percepit feoda induccionum et ea contra formam dicti laudi diuidit ad libitum suum.

of the aforesaid award has required obedience of certain Canons who were installed before the time of the said award.

[11.] Because also the same Dean in processions does not advance straight forward and in a direct line in due order from his own place in the choir, according to the custom of the Church; but across and not in a direct line, sometimes after the officiant of the Office, sometimes by his side, contrary to such custom.

[12.] And because the same Dean withdraws and has long withdrawn a certain chaplain whom he is bound to maintain and find at his own charges for the daily celebration of the Morrow Mass[1] in the said Church.

[13.] Because that the same Dean does not restrain his servants from preventing the gatekeeper of the close from shutting the gates of the close at the proper time as he should do.

[14.] And because the same Dean deprives the Chapter of the jurisdiction over prebends and their prebendaries even after their death, outside the visitatorial power of the Dean, which belongs and pertains to the same Chapter in the case of his absence or neglect.

[15.] Because that also the same Dean withholds from the Chapter 26*s.* 8*d.* which he is bound to pay annually at the celebration of the obit of Henry Lexington[2] in the said Church.

[16.] And because also the same Dean has received the fees of inductions and has divided them at his own will, contrary to the form of the said award.

[1] The special purpose of the Missa matutinalis, which was endowed, was to pray for former Bishops and Deans of Lincoln, and Coventry and Lichfield, and for other Christian souls.

[2] Henry Lexington (brother of John de Lexington, chief justice of the forests north of the Trent) was Bishop of Lincoln 1253—8. His obit was on July 28th or August 8th. In 1440 'the poor chaplains, chantry priests' complained to the Bishop that 3*s.* 10*d.* due for the previous year from that obit was one of those unpaid. *Statutes*, III. 818—9. The Dean eventually had to pay the arrears, which he had withheld for 22 years and which amounted to £29. 6*s.* 3*d.*, to the Cope fund.

[17.] De eo quod idem Decanus prohibet hijs qui Capitulo sunt indebitati, ne Capitulo, vel eorum Nuncio, huiusmodi debita soluant ipsi debitores.

[18.] Quodque idem Decanus subditos in prebendis commorantes, extra tempus visitacionis sue decanalis, ac Canonicos residenciarios et alios habitum in Ecclesia gerentes, ad loca remota extra prebendas huiusmodi, et clausum dicte Ecclesie, ad iudicium vocat et trahit contra consuetudinem et laudum predicta.

[19.] De eo quod idem Decanus diebus capitularibus, ac convencionum Decani et Capituli temporibus, inducit secum in Domum Capitularem familiares suos, et alios seculares et laicos armis invasiuis munitos, qui inibi sedent temporibus Capitulorum et convencionum huiusmodi, ad ipsius Capituli magnum terrorem. cum unus solus virgiarius super custodia hostij capitularis talibus temporibus de consuetudine ecclesie inuigilaret.

[20.] De eo quod idem Decanus, contra consuetudinem et statuta Ecclesie, admittit nonnullos in pauperes clericos, et quasi idiotas[1] in hospicio suo et extra Capitulum, absque aliqua examinacione, vel prestatione obediencie et iuramenti requisiti: similiter et alios ideotas ad habitum in ecclesia admittit nulla examinacione preuia.

[21.] Quodque idem Decanus contra consuetudineȝ ecclesie facit vltimam pulsacionem campanarum ad vesperas et primam cessare ante aduentum executoris officij in chorum.

[22.] De eo quod Decanus fecit chorum expectare aduentum suum postquam executor officij inchoauerit missam suam; in magnum scandalum ecclesie.

[1] Cf. 'conperto quod homines essent sine litteris et idiotae.' *Act. Apost.* iv. 13 (Vulg.).

[17.] Because that the same Dean forbids those who are indebted to the Chapter, [telling] these debtors not to pay their debts to the Chapter or their nuntius[1].

[18.] And because the same Dean summons and drags to judgement, contrary to the aforesaid custom and award, those under him who are sojourning on their prebends, outside the time of his decanal visitation, and Residentiary Canons and others wearing the habit in the Church, to places far distant from their prebends and from the close of the said Church.

[19.] Because that the same Dean on Chapter days and at the times of the assembling of Dean and Chapter, brings with him into the Chapter-House his retainers[2] and other secular and lay persons armed with weapons of offence, who sit there during the times of such Chapter meetings and assemblies to the great intimidation of the Chapter; though only one verger should keep guard over the door of the Chapter-House at such times, according to the custom of the Church.

[20.] Because that the same Dean, contrary to the custom and statutes of the Church, admits certain to be poor clerks, and these, ignorant persons as we might call them, in his own house and not in the Chapter-House, and without any questioning of them on their taking the required promise of obedience and oath; and also likewise he admits other ignorant men to the habit of the Church, without making any previous examination.

[21.] And because the same Dean, contrary to the customs of the Church, causes the bells to cease ringing at evensong and mattins before the entry into the choir of the officiant of the office.

[22.] Because that the Dean has made the choir wait for his own arrival after the celebrant has begun his Mass: to the great scandal of the Church.

1 'nuntius': the official sworn messenger of the Chapter, the 'cursor capituli' called at New College and Winchester the speedy-man. The 'nuncii australis et borealis' were bailiffs or collectors. There was a 'nuncius mortis' civitatis Lincoln.

2 See p. 21, § 15.

[23.] De eo quod Decano sciente et tollerante eius familiares contra nonnullos de habitu ecclesie prosequuntur breuia regia et al[ia]s pro causis que terminari solent ex consuetudine ecclesie in ipsius curia vocata Galilee courte, contra ecclesie libertatem.

[24.] Quodque idem Decanus pro libitu suo aufert ab ecclesia librum eius consuetudinarium vocatum Le blak
* Lf. 2b. boke, qui de consuetudine *Ecclesie semper deberet remanere in vestiario Ecclesie sub custodia thesaurarij.

[25.] Quodque Decanus exigit inspeccionem priuilegiorum et munimentorum ecclesie, quod fieri non debet per quenquam, nisi in presencia Prepositi Canonicorum, et alterius Canonici residensiarij ad hoc per Capitulum assignati.

[26.] De eo quod Decanus impedit Capitulum ne ipsum Capitulum corrigat crimina grauia in absencia vel necligencia Decani; eciam post trinam requisicionem ipsius Decani per Capitulum factam ad ea corrigenda: contra formam dicti laudi.

[27.] Quodque idem Decanus Vicarios in choro per prebendarios rite presentatos, et per Capitulum absente Decano admissos, aliosque ministros ecclesie consimiliter admissos absque iudicio Capituli et cause cognicione, iuris ordine pretermisso, suspendit et priuat.

[23.] Because that with the knowledge and acquiescence of the Dean, his retainers set in motion King's Briefs and so on against certain wearing the habit of the Church, in cases which by the custom of the Church are wont to be settled in its court called the 'Galilee court[1],' contrary to the liberties of the Church.

[24.] And because the same Dean, at his will, takes away from the Church its Consuetudinary called 'The black Book[2],' which by the custom of the Church should always remain in the vestry of the Church under the charge of the Treasurer.

[25.] And because the same Dean insists upon inspecting the privileges and deeds of the Church, which should not be done by anyone except in the presence of the Provost[3] of the Canons and of another Residentiary Canon appointed for this purpose by the Chapter.

[26.] Because that the Dean prevents the Chapter from itself correcting grave offences in the case of the absence or neglect of the Dean: even after three requests made by the Chapter to the Dean to correct them; contrary to the form of the said award.

[27.] And because the same Dean suspends and deprives Vicars duly presented in choir by Prebendaries and admitted in the Dean's absence by the Chapter, and other ministers of the Church admitted in like manner, apart from any decision or cognisance of the matter by the Chapter, in contempt of law and order.

1 The 'Galilee Porch' is at the south-west corner of the great transept. This points to the conclusion that the Galilee Court was most probably held somewhere in this part of the Cathedral Church. There was a coroner, steward, and a constable of the Galilee Court.

2 The Black Book, or '*Liber Niger*,' contains rules regulating the service of the Church and the relative position and duties of the members of the Chapter.

3 The Provost was elected annually. His duty was to look after the business matters of the Chapter and to keep the ordinary seal. There was a Provost of the vicars and a Provost of the poor clerks. It was alleged that in former times there had been two officials, 'praepositus fabricae' and 'praepositus communitatis.'

[28.] De eo quod Decanus, iuxta laudum non vocat canonicos assessores ad sibi assidendum in correccionibus canonicorum detectorum in visitacione sua decanali; et alias per eum faciendis alias non exspectat vocatos; nec vocatorum et presencium requirit consilium contra laudum.

Nota.

[29.] De eo quod Decanus non reuocauit processus quosdam habitos in curia romana et alibi nec eciam bullas et processus impetratos dudum per Magistrum Johannem Shepey Decanum ac alios prout continetur in iuramento per ipsum nunc Decanum in hac parte prestito.

[30.] Quodque idem Decanus ex impetu suo subuertit laudabilem ordinem et regulam chori in festis duplicibus, maiores missas celebrando, cum ad hoc non sit tabulatus, [alios ad hoc] tabulatos perturbando.

[31.] De eo quod idem Decanus plures prebendas in vno die per se, et procuratores suos, visitat; et totidem recipit excessiuas et integras procuraciones absque dispensacione sufficienti[1].

[*inserted above the line.*]

[32.] Quodque idem Decanus non obediuit quibusdam ordinacionibus et declaracionibus per bone memorie Dominum Wyllm Gray nuper Lincoln̄ Episcopum super articulis huiusmodi licium factis; nec eas admittere voluit prout se cum iuramento ordinacioni dicti Episcopi submisit: nec eosdem articulos quos ipsemet Decanus in presencia Thesaurarij Anglie inter se et Capitulum concordatos fore fatebatur, ac ibidem ratificauit et subscripsit, obseruat.

(Bp Gray's Award, dated 27 Sept. 1434.)

[1] See p. 23, and *L. C. S.* II. p. clxx, III. p. 266.

[28.] Because that the Dean, does not summon, as required by the award, Canons to sit with him as assessors in the correction of faults found in Canons at his Decanal Visitation; and otherwise does not wait for those summoned by him for other purposes; and does not ask the opinion of those summoned and present, contrary to the award.

[29.] Because that the Dean has not revoked certain processes advanced in the Roman Curia and elsewhere, nor even the bulls and processes long ago procured by Mr John Shepey[1] the Dean and others, as required by the oath taken in this matter by the present Dean himself.

[30.] And because the same Dean on his own initiative upsets the praiseworthy order and rule of the Choir on double feasts, by celebrating at High Masses when he is not on the table to celebrate them, and by disturbing those who are.

[31.] Because that the same Dean visits several Prebends in one day in person and by his proctors, and takes exorbitant procurations at each place without deduction, and having no sufficient dispensation so to do.

[32.] And because the same Dean has not obeyed certain ordinances and pronouncements made on such matters of strife as these by the Lord William Grey late Bishop of Lincoln, of blessed memory; and would not accept them though he submitted on his oath to the ordinance of the said Bishop; nor does he keep those articles which he, the Dean himself, promised, in the presence of the Treasurer of England, should be agreed upon between himself and the Chapter, and which in the same place he ratified and subscribed[2].

[1] Dr John de Shepey, Dean of Lincoln 1388–1412. Differences arose between him and the Canons which were settled against the Dean by an award made in 1404 by Bp Henry Beaufort, afterwards Cardinal.

[2] The reference here is to Bp Grey's award, 1434 (see the *Chapter Acts*, A. 2. 32; f. 86) which Dr Macworth agreed to accept on oath apparently in the presence of the Treasurer of England. Bp Alnwick however regarded this award as lacking authority owing to some informality in the taking of the submissions of those concerned without their personal attendance, and in his own award, as will be seen later on, annulled it altogether.

[33.] De eo quod idem Decanus magnam partem muri claustri Ecclesie ibidem demoliri, et stabulum vnum super residuam partem muri eiusdem construi fecit, Capitulo inconsulto, et absque eius voluntate, sciencia vel assensu.

[34.] De eo quod idem Decanus non residenciarius exigit sibi responderi et satisfieri de quotidianis distribucionibus; contra consuetudinem ecclesie et formam dispensacionis sue de non residendo.

[35.] Quodque idem Decanus nulla causa legitima subsistente prohibuit Receptori Archidiaconi Lincolñ non suo subdito, ne pauperibus in Hospitali sancti Egidij extra Lincoln' degentibus, sua stipendia persolueret.

[36.] De eo quod idem Decanus, contra laudabilem consuetudinem ecclesie nititur destruere opciones firmarum et
* Lf. 3[a]. hospiciorum ca*nonicalium et presertim in opcione firme canonicalis apud Magnam Bitham; que firma et hospicia haberi debent secundum etatem residencie in ecclesia.

[37.] Quodque idem Decanus nititur expellere a residencia sua procuratorem Capituli missum per ipsum Capitulum ad parliamenta, conuocaciones et alia negocia sua, eo quod idem procurator absens erat ab ecclesia in huiusmodi negocijs.

[38.] De eo quod Decanus contra librum consuetudinarium vsurpat custodiam sigilli communis, quod secundum illum librum remaneret in custodia cancellarij, prepositi et vnius residenciarij ad hoc per Capitulum assignati: qui eciam Cancellarius literas missas Decano et Capitulo coniunctim in Capitulo legeret secundum eundem librum; et tamen Decanus eas preter noticiam Capituli aperit et videt.

[33.] Because that the same Dean, without consulting the Chapter and without its acquiescence, knowledge or consent, caused a large part of the wall of the close of the Church in the same place to be pulled down, and a stable to be built in the remaining portion of the same wall.

[34.] Because that the same Dean, though non-resident, insists that he shall be included and paid in the daily distributions; contrary to the custom of the Church and the form of his dispensation for non-residence.

[35.] And because the same Dean, without any lawful cause, has forbidden the Receiver of the Archdeacon of Lincoln, who is not subject to him, to pay their stipends to the poor men living in the Hospital of St Giles-without-Lincoln.

[36.] Because that the same Dean, contrary to the praiseworthy custom of the Church, strives to annul the options of the Canons' farms and dwelling-houses, and particularly in the case of the option of the Canons' farm at Great Bytham[1]; which farm and dwelling-houses should be held according to one's seniority of residence in the Church.

[37.] And because the same Dean tries to put out of his residence the Proctor of the Chapter, sent by the Chapter itself to Parliament, Convocation and other businesses of the same, on the ground that the same Proctor was away from the Church on these businesses.

[38.] Because that the Dean, contrary to the Consuetudinary book, takes upon himself the charge of the common seal which according to that book should remain in the charge of the Chancellor, Provost, and one Residentiary appointed for this purpose by the Chapter; and the same Chancellor should read, according to the same. book, in Chapter the letters sent to the Dean and Chapter conjointly; and nevertheless the Dean opens and sees these without acquainting the Chapter.

[1] Castle Bytham, or Bytham magna. On the Dean's action as regards this farm see the *Comperta* and *Detecta* at Bp Alnwick's Visitation in 1437. *Statutes* iii. 382, 424–5; cf. *Chapter Acts*, 28 Nov. 1442.

[39.] De eo quod idem Decanus disaduocauit attornatum Capituli in Communi Banco, et promisit breue regium de Recordari[1] fac' exequi per ministros civitatis Lincoln' infra Clausum dicte ecclesie, in magnum preiudicium ecclesie.

[40.] De eo quod idem Decanus non admittit procuratores canonicorum residenciariorum pro tempore absencium.

[41.] Quodque idem Decanus nititur excercere iurisdiccionem per se solum, que per ipsos Decanum et Capitulum coniunctim consueuit et debet excerceri.

[42.] Impedit eciam Capitulum quominus conuocaciones facere, procuratores constituere in negocijs ipsius solius capituli, et insuper quominus Capitulum valeat dispensare in casibus quibus licitum est ei dispensare.

Super quibus omnibus et singulis, ac de vagacione Vicariorum extra chorum tempore diuinorum; de statu fabrice ecclesie videndo et reformando, ac oneribus incumbentibus eidem; de attemptatis per Decanum, pendente visitacione vestra, in eius preiudicium; De capellanis Canonicorum in habitu; De obitu Wyll^{mi} Waltham, et moneta eiusdem; De insinuacionibus et approbacionibus testamentorum, et eorum sequelis fiendis in domo capitulari iudicio Capituli; De minori residencia declaranda; atque alijs quibusdam articulis et grauaminibus pretensis, per dictum Magistrum Johannem Macworth Decanum in ipsius compromisso vel submissione insertis seu inserendis;

[1] 'A writ directed to the Sheriff to remove a cause depending in an inferior court to the King's Bench or Common Pleas is called a *Recordare*, because it commands the Sheriff to make a record of the proceedings (recordare facias loquelam) and to send up the cause.' Giles Jacobs, *Law Dictionary*, 5th edn, 1744, s.v. *Recordare facias loquelam*.

[39.] Because that the same Dean disavowed[1] an attorney of the Chapter in the King's Bench, and undertook to execute a King's Brief 'De recordari' drawn by the officials of the city of Lincoln within the close of the said Church, to the great damage of the Church.

[40.] Because that the same Dean does not admit the proctors of Canons Residentiary temporarily away.

[41.] And because the same Dean tries to exercise jurisdiction by himself alone, although it has been wont to be and ought to be exercised by Dean and Chapter conjointly.

[42.] Also he hinders the Chapter from holding meetings, from appointing proctors for businesses which affect the Chapter alone, and moreover prevents the Chapter dispensing in cases in which it is lawful for it to dispense.

In all and singular which matters, and concerning the straying of the Vicars out of choir in time of Divine Service; concerning the inspecting of the condition of the fabric of the Church and putting the same to rights, and the obligations incumbent upon the same; concerning the things attempted by the Dean to the damage of the same while your visitation was impending; concerning the Canons' chaplains in habit; concerning the obit of William Waltham and the monetary payments connected with the same; concerning probate and administration of wills[2] and of the settlement of the profits thereof in the Chapter House by the decision of the Chapter; concerning the declaring of lesser residence; and certain other articles and charges put forward by the said Mr John Macworth, the Dean, which are set out or shall be set out in his composition or act of

[1] disadvocavit attornatum capituli in communi banco. disadvocare should perhaps be translated 'unbriefed.'

[2] The Ecclesiastical Courts had in their hands until the Reformation the exclusive power of proving wills. At Lincoln the probate of the wills of all members of the Chapter was in the hands of the Dean and Chapter. This right was held by many corporations, e.g. at King's College, Cambridge, the Provost had within the precincts all manner of spiritual and temporal jurisdiction, including the probate of wills.

Alijsque articulis litis vel dissencionis incentiuis, si que occurrerint, si et quando presenti pendente compromisso vestre paternitati, nobisque et dicto Domino Decano, pro bono pacis inter nos reformande expediens visum fuerit, hinc uel inde tradendis: superque ambiguorum dubiorum et obscuritatum tam in prefati Domini Ricardi laudo et presertim terminorum istorum viz. "Excessus," "Communiter," "Insolencia in choro," et aliorum; ac eciam laudorum dudum latorum per bone memorie Dominum Robertum Grostest, et Johannem Dalderby dudum Lincolñ episcopos; et Reuerendum patrem Dominum Henricum Beaufort nuper Lincoln' Episcopum; quam *eciam in libro dicte ecclesie consuetudinario sive registro aut statutis, interpretacione exposicione et declaracione; superque contrariorum, superfluorum, atque illorum que, contrario racionabili et legitimo vsu, aut contrarijs posterioribus statutis in dissuetudinem abierunt, vel reuocate sunt, si que reperiantur, resecacione et evacuacione a libro Registr' et statut' predict', omnium et singulorum premissorum incidentibus et dependentibus; nos canonici residenciarij predicti Capitulum dicte ecclesie facientes, pro nobis et nostris futuris successoribus, vos reuerendum patrem supradictum Arbitrum et Arbitratorem, diffinitorem, arbitralem sententiatorem, et amicabilem compositorem, preceptorem, ordinatorem, dispositorem, pronunciatorem et declaratorem super reformanda pace et concordia in hac parte eligimus et assumimus: et in vos tanquam arbitrum, Arbitratorem, laudatorem, diffinitorem, Arbitralem sentenciatorem et amicabilem Compositorem, preceptorem, ordinatorem, dispositorem, pronunciatorem et declaratorem compromittimus, vt vos alte et basse, absolute et libere, cum cognicione vel sine cognicione cause seu causarum, et de plano ac summarie sine strepitu et figura iudicij possitis inter nos

(The so-called Award of Bp Grosseteste, dated ? 1245; Bp J. de Dalderby's Award, dated 27 July, 1314; Bp Beaufort's Award, dated 30 July, 1404.)

* Lf. 3b.

submission; and all other articles, provoking strife or disagreement, which shall appear, which shall be put forward by one side or the other, if and when it shall seem expedient to you Reverend Father while the present composition is impending, and to us and the said Dean, for the good cause of restoring peace between us; and in the interpretation, explanation, and resolving of ambiguities, doubtful points and obscurities, both in the award of the aforesaid Lord Richard, and in particular of these expressions, "excesses," "in common," and "insolence in choir" and others; and also of the awards put forth in the past by the Lord Robert Grostest, of blessed memory, and John Dalderby, former Bishops of Lincoln; and the Reverend Father the Lord Henry Beawfort, late Bishop of Lincoln[1]; as well as in the "Consuetudinary Book" of the said Church, or "the Register," or Statutes: and concerning the removal and expurgation from the aforesaid Book, Register and Statutes, of things contradictory or superfluous, and of those which through [the growth of] some contrarient [yet] reasonable and legitimate use, or through the enactment of later statutes to the contrary, have fallen into disuse or have been repealed, wherever they may be found; on matters incidental to or arising out of all and singular the foregoing; We the Canons Residentiary aforesaid, making up the Chapter of the said Church, on our own behalf and on behalf of our successors in the future, on our part choose and appoint you the Reverend Father above mentioned as judge and arbitrator, definer, final adjudicator, settler, peacemaker, guide, ordainer, composer, pronouncer and promulgator for the restoration of peace and concord; and to you as judge, arbitrator, awarder, definer, final adjudicator, friendly disposer, guide, ordainer, composer, pronouncer and promulgator we commit [the matter] that you may have power thoroughly, absolutely and freely, with cognition or without cognition of the case or cases, and extrajudicially and summarily,

[1] The award of Bp Grosseteste was made in 1245, that of Bp John de Dalderby in 1314, and that of Cardinal Beaufort in 1404.

et dictum Dominum Decanum semell et pluries, quociens
[Terminus Compromissi.] (*Wednesday, June 24, 1439.*) vobis placuerit ac videbitur expedire, vsque ad festum Natiuitatis sancti Johannis Baptiste, quod erit in Anno Domini M°CCCCXXXIX^no^, super premissis omnibus et singulis, tam virtute huiusmodi submissionis et compromissi, quam vestra ordinaria potestate, arbitrari, laudare, diffinire, arbitraliter sentenciare, precipere, ordinare, disponere ac pronunciare, addere, minuere, corrigere, interpretare, declarare, in scriptis vel sine scriptis, diebus feriatis vel non feriatis, omni hora et loco: nobis tamen canonicis residenciarijs predictis Capitulum vt premittitur facientibus primitus vocatis, et premunitis, et auditis racionibus et allegacionibus nostris, receptisque informacionibus per probaciones et alias iuris vias per nos ministrand', si comparuerimus; in casu quo in termino ad quem fuerimus vocati et premuniti comparere non curaverimus, nobis absentibus, seruato iuris ordine vel non seruato: Promittentes nos pro nobis, nostrisque futuris successoribus canonicis residenciarijs dictis dicte Ecclesie quibuscunque sub pena quacunque spirituali aut temporali censura viz. vel pecuniaria, vel utraque coniunctim, quam in vestro
* Lf. 4^a^. laudo *vel compromisso duxeritis limitandum et assignand', rata et firma semper habere atque tenere, attendere adimplere, et inuiolabiliter obseruare ac in nullo per nos, vel alium seu alios contrafacere vel venire omnibus et singulis que vos per vestrum arbitrium, laudum, arbitratum, mandatum arbitrale, sentenciam arbitralem, ordinacionem, diffinicionem, disposicionem, composicionem, declaracionem, et pronunciationem, arbitranda, laudanda, sentencianda, modo quo supra diffinienda, mandanda, ordinanda, componenda et disponenda, ac eciam addenda, minuenda, corrigenda, interpretanda, et declaranda, quocienscunque duxeritis in premissis, et in quolibet premissorum: Ipsisque omnibus et singulis ac pene vel penis

without the trouble and form of a judgement, between us and the said Lord Dean, once and more often, as often as it shall please you or seem fit, before the Feast of the Nativity of St John Baptist which shall occur in the year 1439, on all and singular the foregoing matters, both by virtue of this act of submission and composition, and by your authority as ordinary, to decide, award, define, finally adjudicate, guide, ordain, settle and make pronouncement, add, take away, correct, interpret, utter, in writing or not in writing, on working days or on holidays, at any hour and place; after however first summoning and forewarning us the Canons Residentiary aforesaid, making up the Chapter aforesaid, and after hearing our reasons and pleas, and after receiving the statements by us to be submitted by means of proofs or other legal methods, if we appear; in any case to which we have been summoned and forewarned and during which we have not troubled to put in an appearance, in our absence, keeping to the order of the law or not keeping to it. We promising on behalf of ourselves and on behalf of our successors in the future the said Canons Residentiary whatsoever of the said Church, under whatsoever spiritual penalty or temporal, that is pecuniary, penalty, or both together, which you in your award or composition shall think fit to fix and appoint, always to hold as valid and binding, to give heed to, to fulfil, and to observe faithfully, and in no case by our own act or by any other or others to act against or contravene all and singular such matters as you by your judgement, award, decision, final decree, adjudication, ordinance, definition, disposition, settlement, promulgation and pronouncement [shall deem necessary] to be adjudicated upon, awarded, decided, defined as above, commanded, ordained, disposed, laid down, and even added to, taken away, put right, explained and promulgated, as often as you shall think fit in the matters afore mentioned, or any one of them; and to give adhesion to, and that immediately on their promulgation, all and singular these decisions even under the penalty or penalties

per vos ordinandis super obseruacione eorundem contra partem reluctantem et non parentem parere et obedire; et mox eis prolatis emologare; Et quod contra vestrum preceptum, laudum, pronunciationem seu arbitrium &c., non appellabimus, nec appellacioneȝ prosequemur; nullum rescriptum et privilegium per nos, vel alium impetrabimus; nec impetratis vtemur; nullam excepcionem opponemus; restitucionem in integrum non petemus; nec illa corrigi seu emendari per superiorem vel aliquem iudicem petemus; Quodque non vtemur cuiuscunque legis vel canonis, statuti, aut consuetudinis beneficio, quod viciet aut infirmare seu viciare valeat huiusmodi compromissum seu arbitrium in totum vel in partem, sive ex persona vestra aut pro personis compromittencium, sive ex forma presentis arbitrij submissionis compromissi, seu ex rebus vel causis de quibus est compromissum, sive ex quacunque alia racione. Ad hec nichilominus spondemus et promittimus quod pena et pene quecunque vna vel plures per vos limitanda seu limitande, semel vel pluries, quociens contra predicta vel aliquod predictorum a nobis seu per nos actum fuerit, vel prefatum laudum seu arbitrium integre obseruatum non fuerit in omnibus et singulis capitulis insolidum committatur et committantur et commissa vel commisse exigatur vel exigantur, qua vel quibus soluta vel solutis, vel non, predicta omnia et singula, et predictum compromissum laudum sive arbitrium in sua permaneant firmitate, et laudo huiusmodi sive arbitrio rato manente, pena nichilominus vel pene peti possit vel possint. Et iuramus nos Canonici residenciarij predicti Capitulum dicte Ecclesie facientes, et iurat nostrum quilibet ad sancta *Euangelia per nos et nostrum quemlibet corporaliter tacta, quod omnia et singula supradicta quatenus nos vel Capitulum dicte Ecclesie concernere poterunt inuiolabiliter obseruabimus et approbabimus: Renunciantes specialiter

Nota pro iuramento Canonicorum.

* Lf. 4[b].

by you to be fixed against that party which holds back and is not ready to obey and submit to them; and that we will not appeal against your ruling, award, pronouncement or judgement, nor will we set appeals on foot; we will procure[1] no rescript or privilege, by our own act or by means of another, nor will we use them if procured; we will make no exception; we will not seek a return to the former state of things; nor will we seek for them to be corrected or altered by any higher, or by any judge at all; and that we will not take advantage of any law, canon, statute or judgement, which shall void or be able to invalidate or void this composition or judgement in whole or in part, arising out of any action on your part or on the part of those who are making the composition; or arising out of the form of the present judgement, act of submission, composition, or arising out of matters and points concerning which the composition is made, or from any other reason whatsoever. With regard to these none the less we promise and undertake that the penalty or penalties, whatsoever they may be, by you to be fixed, once or more often, as often as anything shall be done by us or through us against the aforesaid or any particular point of the aforesaid, or the aforesaid award or judgement shall not be faithfully observed in all and singular its articles absolutely, shall be imposed and if imposed shall be exacted, and whether they be paid or not, all and singular the aforesaid and the aforesaid composition, award or judgement shall remain in full force, and this award or judgement remaining in force, the penalty or penalties none the less shall be able to be exacted.

And we the Canons Residentiary aforesaid making up the Chapter of the said Church do make oath, and each one of us doth make oath before the holy gospels of God which we each one of us have personally touched, that we will faithfully keep and assent to all and singular the aforesaid so far as they can concern us or the Chapter of the said Church: renouncing in particular the benefit of

[1] i.e. from Rome.

legi prohibenti arbitrium fieri cum sacramenti interposicione, et generaliter omni beneficio iuris vel auxilio per quod possemus in totum vel in partem a pena seu ab obseruacione memorati arbitrij sive laudi quomodolibet liberari.

In quorum omnium et singulorum testimonium has nostre submissionis sive compromissi literas sigilli communis capituli predicti appensione ac signo et subscripcione Magistri Roberti Stretton Clerici Ebor dioc' auctoritate apostolica notarij publici fecimus signari.

(Chapter House, *Saturday*, 7 June, 1438.) Data et acta sunt hec in Domo Capitulari ecclesie cathedralis beate Marie Lincolñ supradicte sub Anno Domini MCCCCXXXVIII. Indiccione prima pontificatus Sanctissimi in Christo patris et Domini nostri Domini Eugenij diuina prouidencia huius nominis pape quarti Anno Octavo mensis Junij die Septimo: presentibus tunc ibidem discretis viris Domino Wyll^mo^ Steuenote et Wyll^mo^ Stanlay presbiteris dicte Ecclesie Vicarijs, ac Magistro Wyll^o^ Ryther clerico notario publico, testibus vocatis et rogatis specialiter ad premissa.

¶ Et ego Robertus Stretton, Clericus Ebor dioc',

This notarial mark covers a considerable portion of the written page, and is inserted in the middle of the text. Instead of presuming to copy the '*ne varietur*' mark of his brother notary Robert Stretton, which (no doubt) was before him when he made this transcript, Thomas Colston the scribe of our MS. simply marks its place with *his own* notarial mark.

NOTARIAL MARK OF THOMAS COLSTON, 1439.

any law forbidding our judgement to be made with the intervention of an oath, and in general any legal advantage or assistance by which we might be able to free ourselves in any way whatsoever in whole or in part from penalty or from obedience to the aforesaid judgement or award.

In witness of all and singular of which we have caused these letters of our submission and composition to be signed by the setting thereunto of the common seal of the aforesaid Chapter, and by the signature and subscription of Mr Robert Stretton, Clerk of the Diocese of York, public notary by apostolic authority.

These were given and done in the Chapter House of the Cathedral Church of blessed Mary, of Lincoln aforesaid, in the year of our Lord 1438, in the first indiction of the Pontificate of our most holy Father and Lord in Christ the Lord Eugenius by Divine providence fourth Pope of this name, in the 8th year of his Pontificate, on the 7th day of June; there being present in the same place the worthy Sir William Stevenote and Sir William Stanlay, Priests, Vicars of the same church, and Mr William Ryther, clerk, public notary, who were specially summoned and called as witnesses to the foregoing.

[Here is inserted in the middle of the text the notarial mark of Thomas Colston the scribe of the extant MS. It occurs again at the end of the award. He has put his own mark in the place of the mark of Robert Stretton the scribe of the original MS.]

And I, Robert Stretton, Clerk of the Diocese of York,

publicus sacra auctoritate apostolica Notarius, predictique Capituli ecclesie Lincoln' actorum Capitularium scriba, premissi compromissi et contentorum in eodem prout suprascribuntur per venerabilem virum Magistrum Petrum Partrich dicte ecclesie Lincoln' Cancellarium, et prefati reuerendi Patris Domini Episcopi Lincoln', in quem fit compromissio in ea parte, commissarium ad hoc literatoric deputatum, exibicioni ministracioni et liberacioni factis Capitulo memorato, ipsiusque commissionis ad hoc faciendi, ac tocius compromissi et scripture suprascripte cum copia eiusdem lecture puplice collacioni eorundem, factioni Juramentorum omnium et singulorum canonicorum supranominatorum Domino Wyll^mo^ Derby, Archidiacono Bedeford duntaxat excepto, et eorum quorumlibet, tactis per eos et eorum quemlibet sacrosanctis Dei Euangelijs, de parendo et adimplendo dictum compromissum et scripturam suprascriptum prestacioni, legisque prohibentis arbitrium vel compromissum fieri cum sacramenti interposicione, et omni iuris beneficio, per quod potest

* Lf. 5a. ('Ihc maria' *top margin.*) *penis memorati compromissi liberari, renunciacioni, ceterisque premissis, ut prescribuntur, [quae] sub Anno Domini, Indiccione, pontificatu, mense, die, et loco, proxime suprascriptis, agebantur et fiebant, vnacum prenunciatis testibus presens personaliter interfui, eaque omnia sic fieri vidi et audiui; eaque per alium de voluntate et consensu meis vt premittuntur scripta, de mandato dicti Capituli

public notary by sacred apostolic authority, and scribe of the Chapter acts of the aforesaid Chapter of the Church of Lincoln, of the aforesaid composition and the contents of the same (as they are written out above by the venerable Mr Peter Partrich chancellor of the said church of Lincoln and by his letters for this purpose appointed commissary of the aforesaid Reverend Father the Lord Bishop of Lincoln, to whom the composition was made in this behalf), together with the witnesses aforenamed was personally present at the setting forth rendering and delivery made by the said Chapter; and as scribe of this commission to be made for this purpose, and of the whole composition and the writing above written together with the whole transcript of the same, [was personally present] at the public reading, at the comparison of the same, at the taking of the oath by each and every of the Canons above named (with the exception of Sir William Derby Archdeacon of Bedford), and all of them whatsoever, after they and each one of them had touched the Sacred Gospels of God, swearing to obey and fulfil the said composition and writing above written, and at their renunciation of the power of any law forbidding a judgement or composition to be made with the intervention of an oath, and of the advantage of any law by which it is possible for them to free themselves from the penalties of the said composition; and at the rest of what has gone before as is written out above, and which in the year of our Lord, indiction, pontificate, month, day and place, last named above, were done and took place; and together with the witnesses aforenamed I was personally present, I saw and I heard all particulars so taking place; and these things written out by another with my freewill and consent as they occur above, by the command of the said Chapter I have made public and have reduced them to

publicaui, et in hanc publicam formam redegi; Signoque et nomine meis solitis et consuetis, vna cum appensione Sigilli communis ad causas ipsius Capituli signaui; et me hic subscripsi in fidem et testimonium omnium prescriptorum. Et constat michi notario prescripto de interlineari harum diccionum facta "Absensque sic pascere[1]" inter vij et viij lineas, ac diccionis "Demoliri[2]," diccionisque "Tricessimo[3]" superius interlineate; quas approbo, et suspicione sinistra carere desidero atque volo: Et constat michi eciam de interlineari huius diccionis "Renunciacioni[4]" facta in subscripcione prescrip' quam approbo et cetera.

(ii.) *Iħu maria.*

Reverendo in Christo Patri ac domino Domino Wyllm̄o Dei gracia Lincolñ Episcopo, vester humilis et deuotus Johannes Macworth Decanus Ecclesie vestre Lincolñ, obedienciam si et quatenus de iure debeatur, et omnimode reuerencie plenitudinem cum honore debit' tanto Patri.

Cum iampridem nonnullis litibus, controversijs ac discordijs inter Decanos Ecclesie Lincoln' predecessores meos ac subsequenter me Johannem Decanum predictum ex vna parte, confratres suos et meos Capitulum eiusdem ecclesie ex altera, in Romana Curia, et alibi in iudicio et extra iudicium, sumptuosis quam plurimum agitatis; per laudum et arbitrium venerabilis patris Ricardi nuper Episcopi Lincoln' predecessoris vestri vigore compromissi in ipsum venerabilem patrem hinc inde facti sopitis; alie graues et scandalose inter me Decanum et Capitulum

[1] This occurs on p. 56 l. 22 *of this edition.*

[2] On p. 68 l. 2 above.

[3] On p. 78 l. 13 above (in the date).

[4] On p. 80 l. 20.

this public form; and I have signed them with my usual and accustomed signature and name together with the attachment of the Chapter's common seal "ad causas[1]," and here I have subscribed my name in proof and evidence of all above written. And the underlining of the following words is due to me the notary aforesaid:—"absensque sic pascere" between the 7th and 8th lines; and of the word "demoliri" and of the word "tricessimo" interlined above: which I acknowledge and desire and wish to be free from any suspicion of tampering[2]; and there is also due to me the interlining of this word "Renunciacioni" made in the subscription before written, which I acknowledge, and so forth.

Jesus Mary.

(ii) TO THE REVEREND FATHER and Lord in Christ, the Lord WILLIAM by the grace of God Bishop of Lincoln, your humble and devoted John Macworth, Dean of your Church of Lincoln, obedience if and so far as it is due by law and the fulness of all manner of reverence and honour due to so great a Father.

The Dean's case and his complaints.

WHEREAS some time ago divers strifes, quarrels and differences, between the Deans of the Church of Lincoln my predecessors, and eventually between me John the Dean aforesaid on the one side, and their brethren, and my own, the Chapter of the same Church on the other side, pursued in the Roman Curia and elsewhere, in court and out of court at very great expense, were allayed by the award and judgement of the venerable Father Richard late Bishop of Lincoln your predecessor, in virtue of the composition made by both parties to that venerable Father; yet other grievous and scandalous issues have again arisen between me the Dean and the Chapter (by

[1] *sigillum ad causas*: Such seals were distinguished on the one hand from the 'great seals' or seals of dignity with their counterseals, and on the other from private seals (*secreta*). The seal *ad causas* was used for public instruments of a less important nature than those for which the seal of dignity was reserved. At Lichfield the seals *ad causas et negotia* were properly in the Chancellor's custody. *Statutes*, ii. 25; cf. ii. 34.

[2] See notes on p. 82.

ipsum illo procurante qui a principio sue ruine vnitatem ecclesie rescindere, et caritatem vulnerare invidie sue felle indies conatur, denuo suscitentur questiones:

[1.] De et super eo, quod ipsum Capitulum Ecclesie in litibus et querelis quas in curijs spiritualibus voluntarie contra me Decanum, non ad vtilitatem Ecclesie, quin verius in ipsius graue dispendium et scandalum, mouet et mouere consueuit[1],

[*Parker has written in the margin* 'Decanus iure prebende residentiam facit canonicalem.'] Vna cum ipso in expensis contribuere contra meipsum, tam ad quantum quilibet ipsius Capituli Canonicus in ea parte oneratur de distribucionibus et alijs pecuniarum summis michi, racione mee residencie canonicalis quam in ipsa ecclesia iure prebende mee de Nassyngton quam obtineo in eadem, debitis, subtrahendo et defalcando.

[2.] Ac quod Prepositus ecclesie Lincolñ predicte pro tempore existens in voluntarijs et inutilibus huiusmodi litibus
* Lf. 5b. quando contingunt, pecunias cum quibus ministris *dicte ecclesie in diuinis officiantibus et ministrantibus pro ipsorum necessario victu satisfaceret, ex ipsius Capituli precepto me Decano aliquociens inconsulto, et quandoque inuito et prohibente dissipat et consumit.

[3.] Quodque Capitulum predictum feoda, annuas pensiones, et confirmaciones, atque concessiones iurium et bonorum dicte ecclesie tam Clericis quam laicis, procuratorum et attornatorum constituciones, et alia gesta sub nomine Decani et Capituli me Decano irrequisito et ignorante cum eis placuerit faciunt, et sic facere non omittunt.

[4.] Ipsum insuper Capitulum, ordinaciones, dispensaciones, et statuta, contra consuetudines, ritus, obseruancias racionabiles, et statuta antiqua ipsius ecclesie, atque laudum

[1] There is a full-stop, or point, after '*consueuit*' in our MS.; but it seems here (as oftentimes) to have only the value of a comma.

the machinations of him who from the beginning of his fall strives day by day more and more to rend the unity of the Church, and to wound charity by the gall of his own envy), concerning and over the following points:

[1.] That as a body the Chapter of the Church in strifes and accusations which it sets in motion, and has been wont to set in motion in the spiritual courts wilfully[1] against me the Dean, not to the benefit of the Church, but more truly to the grievous expense and scandal of it,

The Chapter, I say, [makes me][2] contribute along with itself in paying costs against myself by subtracting and deducting from the distributions and other sums of money that are due to me, both in virtue of my canonical residence, up to the amount for which each Canon of the Chapter is liable in that respect, as also [from those due] even in the [rectorial] church itself which I hold in Nassington by right of my prebend there.

[2.] And that the Provost of the aforesaid Church of Lincoln for the time being scatters and wastes in vexatious cases and useless litigation[1] the monies which he should expend on the ministers of the said Church who officiate and serve at Divine Service, in their necessary maintenance, by mandate of the Chapter alone without consulting me the Dean, and sometimes when I object and forbid it.

[3.] And that the aforesaid Chapter assign whenever it pleases them and do not cease so to assign, fees, annual pensions, confirmations, and concessions of the rights and goods of the said Church both to clerks and laymen, appoint proctors and attorneys and perform other acts in the name of the Dean and Chapter without asking my permission and without the knowledge of me the Dean.

[4.] Moreover the Chapter has put forth and made ordinances, dispensations and statutes contrary to the customs, rites, reasonable observances and ancient statutes of the Church itself, and contrary to the award above mentioned

[1] *voluntarie...in voluntariis litibus*; wilfully...in irresponsible, unauthorised, wilful litigation. See below, p. 103, in the 2nd article of the Award itself.

[2] It will be observed that we translate as if *cogit me*, or *facit me*, had been intended, but had accidentally dropped out. [Can *contribuere* = *contribuerunt*, or else may it be translated 'to assess me'? R. M. W.]

superius memoratum eciam iuramento vallatum me Decano inconsulto edidit atque fecit; et sic edere et facere non formidat.

[5.] Cumque eciam canonici singuli ipsius ecclesie in ipsa residenciam facientes canonicalem, iuxta statuta et consuetudines eiusdem ecclesie, debeant habere singulos capellanos sive clericos honestos suis sumptibus qui in habitu chori ipsos canonicos in ingressu Chori et Capituli sequantur, et ipsis circa summum altare in diuinis, et in altarium incensacionibus ministrent; Nonnulli tamen predicte ecclesie canonici residenciarij se predictis statutis et consuetudinibus nullatenus astrictos fore pretendentes, capellanos seu clericos huiusmodi habere non curant; sed vicarios de choro aut Cantariarum Capellanos, seu alios chori clericos in cantu et ad aliter in diuinis officiandum periciores et ydoneores ad huiusmodi ministeria eis impendenda euocant et educunt; in diuini cultus diminucionem manifestam.

[6.] Et quod cantarias perpetuas in ipsa ecclesia vacantes Capitulum predictum lucris illicitis et indebitis inhians et innitens conferre aut conferri facere non curat; sed earum fructus et redditus, contra ipsarum fundatorum pias voluntates, sibi retinet, et in suos vsus dampnabiliter conuertit.

[7.] Item quod legata ad vsus certos et determinatos ex pijs quorundam testatorum disposicionibus dicte ecclesie relicta Capitulum predictum in vsus alios, et quandoque inutiles contra ipsorum moriencium voluntates, sua propria temeritate conuertit et exponit.

[8.] Item quod fructus, redditus et prouentus quarundam in Ecclesia cantariarum per bone memorie Philippum quondam Episcopum Lincolñ propter ipsarum exilitatem vnitarum, non in exhibicionem capellanorum, sed contra

although it is safeguarded by an oath, without consulting me the Dean; and does not fear so to put forth and make them.

[5.] And whereas also each Canon of this Church keeping canonical residence in it, according to the custom and statutes of the same Church, should have each a Chaplain or respectable Clerk at their own charges to follow in their choir habit the Canons themselves at their entry into choir and Chapter house, and to serve them about the High Altar in Divine worship and at the censings of the Altars, nevertheless certain Canons Residentiary of the aforesaid Church, claiming that they should not be bound in anywise by the aforesaid statutes and customs, do not trouble themselves to have Chaplains or Clerks: but summon and draw away choir Vicars or chantry Chaplains or other Clerks of the choir skilled rather in singing or more fit to perform certain other offices of Divine Service, to lay these duties upon them; to the manifest lowering of the standard of Divine Worship.

[6.] And that the Chapter aforesaid gaping for and grasping after unlawful and undue profits does not fill nor cause to be filled the perpetual Chantryships in the Church when vacant; but itself retains their fruits and incomes contrary to the pious intentions of the founders of the same, and damnably converts them to its own uses.

[7.] Also that the Chapter aforesaid in its audacity turns and converts legacies left for definite and fixed objects to the said Church by the pious dispositions of certain testators, to other and sometimes useless objects contrary to the intentions of the deceased themselves.

[8.] Also that the Chapter aforesaid has divided and distributed the fruits, returns, and incomes of certain Chantries in the Church, which were united on account of their slenderness [of endowment] by Philip, formerly Bishop of Lincoln of blessed memory[1], not in the maintenance of

[1] Philip de Repingdon at one time Chancellor of Oxford and a sympathiser with Wiclif, but later Chaplain to the King, Bishop of Lincoln 1408–1419, and Cardinal (1408), and a stern repressor of Lollardism. He resigned his bishopric in 1419 and died in 1424.

(The union of small chantries by Bp Repingdon.) * Lf. 6[a].

fundationem cantariarum predictarum, et predictam vnionem, Capitulum predictum veluti bona ipsius communia, conferendo inter canonicos residenciarios diuidit, et distribuit, et sic a tempore huiusmodi vnionis diuisit; *me Decano renitente et reclamante.

[9.] Item quod Canonici residenciarij nonnulli panno quem de camera communi pro pauperibus induendis iuxta ecclesie consuetudinem recipiunt, seipsos et suos quandoque vestiunt, hoc sibi licere asserentes.

[10.] Item quod Capitulum predictum inter cetera de facto statuerunt, licet nulliter, quod in minori residencia nullus dicte ecclesie Canonicus stare valeat, nisi prius maiorem inibi fecerit residenciam per triennium; me Decano et Canonico ad tunc et adhuc residenciario minime ad hoc vocato.

[11.] Item quod michi Decano inspeccioneȝ privilegiorum et munimentorum dicte ecclesie ac liberum introitum ad repositorium eorundem denegant minus iuste.

['Quia decanus sede vacante obijcit canonicis, Nota laudum Alnwici in medio folij de decano presenti ad tale signum—' *Parker*.]

[12.] Item quod nonnulli canonici sede ipsius ecclesie vacante in officiales Lincolñ iuxta ordinacionem in ea parte factam assumpti, ius meum decanale sibi vsurpant; canonicos in ipsam ecclesiam inducendo; ecclesias de communa visitando; procuraciones recipiendo; et in me seu in alium dicte ecclesie Decanum jurisdiccioneȝ habere et exercere posse vendicando.

[13.] Item quod predictum Capitulum me Decano inconsulto, aut non consenciente, lites et acciones nomine Decani et Capituli, seu Ecclesie nomine, suscitant et intentant.

[14.] Item quod Canonici primo ad residenciam venientes hospicia eis assignata reparare aut reficere non curant, sed ea ruere permittunt, propter spem ad alia migrandi

Chaplains but contrary to the foundation of the aforesaid Chantries and the aforesaid union, as if they were the common property of the Chapter itself, by bestowing them among the Canons Residentiary, and has so divided them from the date of such union in spite of the opposition and resistance of me the Dean.

[9.] Also that certain Canons Residentiary sometimes clothe themselves and their households, asserting that they are allowed to do so, with the cloth which they receive from the common room for the clothing of the poor according to the custom of the Church.

[10.] And that the Chapter aforesaid among other things has actually determined, although it is beyond its powers, that no Canon of the said Church shall be able to be in lesser residence in it, unless he shall have first kept in it greater residence for a period of three years; without summoning for this purpose me the Dean, and Canon then and still residentiary.

[11.] Also that they unjustly refuse to me the Dean the right of inspecting the privileges and muniments of the said Church, and free access to the room where the same are kept.

[12.] Also that divers Canons, when the see of this Church is vacant, appointed as officials of Lincoln according to the ordinances made in such case, take upon themselves the exercise of my powers as Dean by inducting Canons into the Church, by visiting Churches belonging to the common body, by receiving fees, and by claiming that they have and can exercise jurisdiction over me or any other Dean of the said Church.

[13.] Also that the aforesaid Chapter without consulting me the Dean, and without my consent, set in motion and persist in litigation and actions, in the name of the Dean and Chapter, or in the name of the Church.

[14.] Also that Canons when they first come into residence do not trouble to put in order and renovate the dwelling houses assigned to them but allow them to fall into disrepair in the hope of removing to others when they fall

cum vacauerint; in tantum quod mansiones canonicorum infra clausum ecclesie eo pretextu multum sunt ruinose et defectiue.

Super quibus omnibus et singulis, atque alijs quibusdam articulis et grauaminibus pretensis per presidentem et capitulum dicte ecclesie in ipsorum compromisso vel submissione insertis seu inserendis; alijsque articulis litis, vel dissencionis incentiuis si que occurrerint, si et quando presenti pendente compromisso, vestre paternitati, michique et dictis presidenti et Capitulo, pro bono pacis inter nos reformande expediens visum fuerit hinc vel inde tradendis; Necnon super ambiguorum dubiorum et obscuri-
[*underlined*] tatum · tam in prefati Domini Ricardi laudo, *quam eciam in libro dicte ecclesie consuetudinario siue Registro*, aut Statutis, interpretacione exposicione et declaracione; ipso tamen Laudo in sui essencialibus et substancialibus
['Nota protestacionem decani.' *P*.] illibato et illeso manente, de quo protestor; Superque contrariorum superfluorum, atque illorum que contrario racionabili et legitimo vsu, aut contrarijs posterioribus statutis in dissuetudinem abierunt, vel reuocate sunt, si que reperiantur, reseruacione[1] et euacuacione a libro registro et statutis predictis omniumque et singulorum premissorum incidentibus et dependentibus:

Ego Johannes Decanus predictus pro me et meis futuris successoribus, vos reuerendum patrem supradictum
* Lf. 6b. *arbitrum et· arbitratorem, laudatorem, et diffinitorem, summatorem et amicabilem compositorem, preceptorem, ordinatorem, dispositorem, pronunciatorem, et declaratorem super reformanda pace et concordia in hac parte eligo et assumo; et in vos tanquam arbitrum, et arbitratorem, laudatorem, diffinitorem, arbitralem sentenciatorem, et amicabilem compositorem, preceptorem, ordinatorem, dispositorem, pronunciatorem, et declaratorem compromitto vt vos alte et basse, absolute ac libere, cum cognicione vel sine cognicione cause seu causarum et de

[1] *reseruacione* :—Perhaps we should read 'resecacione,' as in the corresponding 'compromise' on p. 72 above.

vacant; to such an extent that the Canons' houses within the close of the Church are for this reason in a very ruinous and defective state.

Upon which matters, all and singular, and on certain other articles and charges put forward by the President and Chapter of the said Church, which have been set out or shall be set out in their composition or act of submission, and certain other articles causing strife and dissension should any such appear; to be put forward by one side or the other if and when it shall seem expedient to your Paternity, while the composition is impending, and to me and to the said President and Chapter; for the good cause of restoring peace between us; moreover in the interpretation explanation and resolving of ambiguities, doubtful points and obscurities, both in the award of the aforesaid Lord Richard and also in the book called the "Consuetudinary Book" of the same Church or "Register," or statutes; the said award none the less remaining in its substance or essentials unimpaired and unharmed, on behalf of which book I make my protest; and in the removal and expurgation[1] from the aforesaid book, register, and statutes, of things contradictory or superfluous, and of those things which in virtue of some different reasonable and legitimate usage or through the enactment of later statutes to the contrary have fallen into disuse; on matters incidental to or arising out of all and singular the foregoing:

I, John the Dean aforesaid, on behalf of myself and my successors after me, on my part choose and accept you the Reverend Father above mentioned as judge and arbitrator, awarder, definer, consummator, and peacemaker, guide, ordainer, settler, pronouncer and promulgator, for the restoration of peace and concord; and to you as judge and arbitrator, awarder, definer, final adjudicator and peacemaker, guide, ordainer, settler, pronouncer and promulgator, I commit the matter, that you may have power thoroughly, absolutely, and freely, with cognition or without cognition of the case or cases, and extrajudicially and

[1] resecacione (*al.* reservacione) et euacuacione.

plano ac summarie, sine strepitu et figura iudicij, possitis inter me ac dictos presidentem et capitulum semel et pluries quociens vobis placuerit ac videbitur expedire, vsque ad festum Nativitatis Sancti Johannis Baptiste quod erit in Anno Domini MCCCCXXXIX°.

Super omnibus premissis et singulis tam virtute huius submissionis et compromissi quam vestra ordinaria potestate, arbitrari laudare, diffinire, arbitraliter sentenciare, precipere, ordinare, disponere et pronunciare, addere, minuere, corrigere, interpretari, declarare in scriptis vel sine scriptis, diebus feriatis vel non feriatis, omni hora et loco me tamen Decano predicto primitus vocato et premunito et auditis racionibus et allegacionibus meis · (*sic.*) receptisque informacionibus per l probaciones et alias vias iuris per me ministrandis, si comparuero · et in casu quo in termino ad quem fuero vocatus vel premunitus comparere non curauero me absente servato iuris ordine vel non servato. Promittens me pro me, meisque futuris successoribus Decanis ecclesie predicte quibuscunque, sub pena quacunque spirituali aut temporali censura, videlicet vel pecuniaria vel utraque coniunctim quam in vestro laudo vel compromisso duxeritis limitandam et assignandam, rata et firma semper habere atque tenere, attendere, adimplere et inuiolabiliter obseruare ac in nullo per me, vel alium aut alios contrafacere vel venire omnia et singula, que vos per vestrum arbitrium, laudum, arbitratum, mandatum arbitrale, sentenciam arbitralem, ordinacionem, diffinicionem, disposicionem, composicionem, et pronunciacionem arbitranda, laudanda, summanda, modo quo supra diffinienda, mandanda, ordinanda, componenda et disponenda; ac eciam addenda, minuenda, corrigenda, interpretanda et declaranda quocienscunque duxeritis in premissis, et in quolibet premissorum; Ipsisque omnibus et singulis, ac pena vel penis per vos ordinandis super obseruacioneȝ eorundem contra partem reluctantem et non parentem parere et obedire, et mox eis prolatis

summarily, without the noise and form of a judgement, between me and the said Provost and Chapter, once, or more, so often as it shall please you or seem fit, before the Feast of the Nativity of St John Baptist which shall occur in the year 1439.

On all and singular the foregoing matters both by virtue of this act of submission and composition and by your authority as Ordinary, to decide, award, define, finally adjudicate, guide, ordain, settle, and make pronouncement, add, take away, correct, interpret, utter, in writing or not in writing, on holidays and working days, at any hour and place, after however first summoning and forewarning me the aforesaid Dean and hearing my reasons and pleas: and after receiving the statements by me to be submitted by means of proofs and other legal methods if I appear; and in case I shall not have taken pains to put in an appearance within the time for which I have been summoned and forewarned, [then] in my absence, keeping to the order of the law or not keeping to it. Promising on my own behalf, and on behalf of my successors in the future of the aforesaid Church, under whatsoever spiritual penalty, or temporal that is pecuniary censure, or both together, which you in your award or composition shall think fit to fix and appoint, always to hold as valid and binding, to give heed to, to fulfil and faithfully observe, and in no case by my own act, or by any other or others, to act against or contravene all and singular such matters as you by your judgement, award, decision, final decree, adjudication, ordaining, definition, disposition, settlement and pronouncement [shall deem necessary] to be adjudicated upon, awarded, decided, defined as above, commanded, ordained, disposed and laid down, and even added to, taken away, corrected, explained and promulgated, as often as you shall think fit in the matters afore mentioned or any one of them; and to give adhesion to, and that immediately on their promulgation, all and singular these decisions and to the penalty or penalties by you to be fixed against that party which holds back and is not ready to obey and submit to them;

* Lf. 7a. emologare. Et quod contra *vestrum preceptum, laudum pronunciacionem seu arbitrium non appellabo, nec appellacionem prosequar; nullum rescriptum vel privilegium per me vel alium impetrabo, nec impetratis vtar; nullam excepcionem apponam; restitucionem in integrum non petam; nec illa corrigi seu emendari per superiorem, vel aliquem iudicem petam; quodque non vtar cuiuscunque legis vel canonis statuti aut consuetudinis beneficio quod viciet seu infirmare vel viciare valeat huiusmodi compromissum; seu[1] ex rebus vel causis de quibus est compromissum, siue ex quacunque alia racione. Ad hec nichilominus spondeo et promitto quod pena et pene quecunque vna vel plures, per vos limitanda vel limitande semel vel pluries quociens contra predicta vel aliquod predictorum a me seu per me actum fuerit, vel prefatum laudum seu arbitrium integre obseruatum non fuerit in omnibus et in singulis capitulis insolidum committatur et committantur, et commissa vel commisse exigatur vel exigantur, qua vel quibus soluta vel solutis, vel non predicta omnia et singula, et predictum compromissum laudum seu arbitrium in sua permaneant firmitate; et laudo huiusmodi siue arbitrio rato manente; pena nichilominus sive pene peti possit et possint.

[Nota iuramentum decani.] Et juro ad hec sancta dei euangelia per me corporaliter tacta, quod Ego Johannes Decanus predictus omnia et singula supradicta, quatenus me ad meum decanatum coniunctim vel diuisim concernere poterunt, inuiolabiliter obseruabo et approbabo renuncians specialiter legi prohibenti arbitrium fieri cum facta sacramenti interposicione; et generaliter omni beneficio iuris vel auxilio per quod possim in totum vel in partem a pena seu ab obseruacione memorati arbitrij siue laudi quomodolibet liberari.

In quorum omnium et singulorum testimonium has mee submissionis sive compromissi literas mei sigilli decanalis appensione, ac Signo et subscripcione Magistri

[1] Some words, similar to the corresponding clauses on p. 76, lines 12–17, may have dropped out of the text here.

and that I will not appeal against your ruling, award, pronouncement or judgement, nor will I set an appeal on foot; I will procure no rescript or privilege by my own act or by any other, nor will I use them if such be procured; I will offer no exception; I will not seek a return to the former state of things[1], nor will I seek for those things to be corrected or altered by any higher or by any judge at all; and that I will not take advantage of any law, canon, statute or custom, which shall void or be able to invalidate or void this composition, either [by occasion of the form of the present judgement, act of submission, or composition; or][2] by any of those matters or points concerning which this composition is made, or for any other reason whatsoever. Furthermore, none the less, I promise and undertake that the penalty or penalties whatsoever they may be, by you to be fixed once or more often, as often as anything shall be done by me or through me against the aforesaid or any particular point of the aforesaid, or the aforesaid award or judgement shall not be faithfully observed in all and singular its articles absolutely, shall be imposed, and if imposed shall be exacted, and whether they be paid or not, in all and singular the aforesaid, and the aforesaid composition award and judgement shall remain in full force, and this award or judgement remaining in force it shall be possible none the less to exact the penalty or penalties.

And I swear to this, touching the Holy Gospels of God, that I John the Dean aforesaid will faithfully observe and assent to all and singular the aforesaid so far as they can concern me in respect of my office as Dean, renouncing in particular the benefit of any law forbidding a judgement to be made with the intervention of an oath; and in general any legal advantage or assistance by which I might be able to free myself in any way whatsoever, in whole or in part, from the penalty, or from obedience to the aforesaid judgement or award.

In witness whereof, all and singular, I have caused these letters of my submission and composition to be signed by the setting thereunto of my seal as Dean, and

[1] *restitutionem in integrum:* possibly 'restitution in full.'

[2] See the note opposite; and cf. p. 77.

Thome Atkyn Clerici Covent. et Lych. dioceseos auctoritate Appostolica notarij publici feci consignari[1].

(Nassington, *Monday*, June 16, 1438.) Data et acta sunt hec apud Nassyngton Anno Domini MCCCCXXX°VIIJ°. Indiccione prima Sanctissimi in Christo patris et domini nostri Eugenij diuina prouidencia huius nominis pape quarti, Anno octauo, mensis Junij die sextodecimo presentibus tunc ibidem discretis viris domino Thoma Cokayn Capellano, et Ricardo Ireton domicello Lincoln̄. Covent. et Lich. dioceseos, testibus vocatis et rogatis specialiter ad premissa.

* Lf. 7[b]. ¶ Et ego Thomas Atkyn Clericus Couent. et *Lich. dioceseos publicus autoritate Apostolica notarius premissis omnibus et singulis dum sic sub Anno Domini, Indiccione pontificatu, mense die et loco predictis agebantur et fiebant vna cum prenominatis testibus, presens personaliter interfui · eaque sic fieri vidi et audiui scripsi, publicaui, et in hanc publicam formam redegi, meque hic subscripsi ac signo et nomine meis solitis et consuetis signari rogatus in fidem et testimonium vt omnium premissorum.

Nos igitur Willielmus Episcopus predictus qui finem imponere litibus affectamus, sed precipue membris corporis mistici cuius licet immeriti sumus caput; huiusmodi compromissis receptis nonnullisque articulis pro bono pacis per ipsas partes vtrinque et ex mutuo eorum consensu nobis datis et productis coram nobis testibus in non modico numero, instrumentis et euidenciis et alijs exhibitis a partibus hinc et inde ac ipsis post modum publicatis, et eorum copia partibus decreta auditis eciam

[1] The office of notary was conferred on T. Atkyn by a faculty from Pope Martin V., Feb. 7, 1420, subject to examination by [J. Macworth] the Dean of Lincoln. (*Cal. Papal Letters*, vii. p. 147.)

by the signature and subscription of Mr Thomas Atkyn clerk of the diocese of Coventry and Lichfield and public notary by apostolic authority.

These were given and done at Nassyngton in the year of our Lord 1438 in the first indiction of our most holy Father and Lord Eugenius by Divine Providence fourth Pope of this name, in the 8th year of his pontificate on the 16th day of the month of June, there being present the worthy Sir Thomas Cockayn, chaplain, and Richard Ireton *Domicellus*[1], in Lincoln, of the diocese of Coventry and Lichfield, who were specially called and summoned as witnesses to the foregoing.

And I Thomas Atkyn, clerk of the diocese of Coventry and Lichfield, public notary by apostolic authority, together with the aforenamed witnesses, was present in person at all and singular the foregoing while they were then being taken in hand and done, in the aforesaid year of our Lord, indiction, pontificate, month, day and place; and these things I saw and heard so to be done; I have written them down, I have published and reduced them to this public form, and have here subscribed myself both by my accustomed signature and name, and have signed, as requested, in witness and testimony of all the foregoing.

WE THEREFORE the said Bishop William who purpose to put an end to strifes, and specially for members of that mystical body whose head we are, although unworthy, having received such compositions, and after several articles in the interest of peace had been given by mutual consent on either side by the parties themselves concerned, and witnesses in no small number had been produced, instruments, evidences and so forth exhibited by the parties on either side and these had been made public afterwards, and a copy decreed [? directed] for the parties,

[1] *domicellus*: a chamberlain or page. The word was sometimes applied to the young son of a nobleman. Ric. Ireton is described as 'serviens decani' in one of the allegations made by Ric. Ingoldesby, one of the Canons Residentiary at Bishop Alnwick's visitation in 1437. (Bradshaw and Wordsworth's *Statutes*, iii. 391.)

responsionibus tam ad articulos, pendentibus huiusmodi compromissis, nobis datos, quam in ipsis compromissis comprehensos, per partes easdem hinc inde factis; considerantes et excogitantes quod *id quod omnes tangit ab omnibus debet approbari;* et ne quis confratrum nostrorum dignitates personatus aut prebendas in ipsa ecclesia nostra optinencium et ne aperte possit conqueri se contemptum; et alijs ex causis nos moventibus; ad certum diem in Capitulo ejusdem ecclesie eosdem omnes et singulos fecimus conuocari: quibus dictis die et loco aliquibus, videlicet personaliter, et nonnullis per eorum procuratores comparentibus, dicta compromissa exposuimus: qui sigillatim interrogati per nos, eisdem compromissis vnanimiter consenserunt et eadem rata firma atque grata et accepta habuerunt; petentes ut iuxta nobis in hac parte traditam potestatem procedere curaremus.

VNDE nos Wyllelmus Episcopus predictus visis testium omnium hinc inde productorum attestacionibus et euidenciis memoratis; ac ipsis partibus multis diebus ipsis (*sic.*) ad nos informandum assignatis; iurisque alligacionibus et disputacionibus auditis; et nobiscum, ac aliorum cum quibus communicauimus, deliberacione prehabita diligenti: vocatis quoque partibus supradictis § arbitrium, laudum, mandatum, et arbitralem sentenciam audiendum; eisque coram nobis ad hoc specialiter *constitutis, ad laudem omnipotentis Dei qui est pacis auctor et amator, Preceiseque eius genitricis gloriose videlicet virginis Marie Patrone nostre, ex cuius thalamo processit in orbem, qui venit pacem dare gentibus, et in cuius honore ipsa ecclesia

§ *Later* MSS. *insert* 'ad'.

* Lf. 8[a].

rejoinders heard as well to articles presented to us while such compositions were pending, as also to those articles which are embodied in the compositions themselves which have been made by the same parties on either side; We considering and bethinking us that 'what concerns all ought to have the consent of all,' and lest any of our brother-canons who have obtained dignities, offices as *Personae*, or prebends in this our Church, lest, I say, he should be able openly to complain that he has been disregarded, as well as from other causes influencing us thereto, have caused all and singular the same to be called together on a certain day in the chapter-house of the same Church; at which day and place aforesaid to some appearing personally and to other some by their proctors we did make known the aforesaid compositions; and they being questioned by us one by one unanimously assented to the same compositions, and accepted them as ratified and established, approved and received, praying us that in accordance with the power committed to us in this behalf we would make it our business to proceed.

The beginning of the Award.

WHEREFORE We Bishop William aforesaid after seeing the testimony of the witnesses brought forward by both parties and the evidences above mentioned, and after these many days have been reserved for these parties to give us information; after hearing also the legal pleadings and arguments, and after careful consideration by ourself and with others whom we have consulted; and after summoning the parties aforesaid to hear our decision, award, injunction, and adjudication; and they being specially gathered together in our presence for this purpose, to the praise of Almighty God who is the author and lover of peace and of his exalted Mother the glorious Virgin Mary our Patroness, from whose womb came He forth into the world who came to give peace to the nations, and to whose honour this Church of ours was built

nostra constructa est et dedicata est; sicut arbiter, arbitrator, laudator, et sicut amicabilis compositor, et sicut parcium et loci huiusmodi ordinarius et Episcopus; ex virtute et forma compromissorum predictorum et omni modo et iure quo melius possumus viam arbitratoris, laudatoris et amicabilis compositoris sequentes, dicimus, arbitramur, laudamus, diffinimus, arbitraliter sentenciamus, mandamus, ordinamus, disponimus et pronunciamus.

1 = *D.* 1. [‘*D*’, followed by a numeral, refers to the *Dean's* complaints against the Canons. *Supra* pp. 85—91.]

IN PRIMIS VIDELICET, vt cum Decanus dicte ecclesie [quiscunque], in ea canonicus prebendatus vice duorum, Decani videlicet et canonici prebendati fungitur[1]: prefatus Magister Johannes Decanus modernus canonicus prebendatus in eadem ecclesia, et quiscunque futurus Decanus eiusdem ecclesie canonicus prebendatus in eadem, singuli quoque alij canonici eiusdem ecclesie prebendati residenciarij; in omnibus causis placitis negocijs et querelis pro parte capituli, et contra ipsum capitulum motis et mouendis de porcione, que ipsum Decanum vt Canonicum prebendatum et non vt Decanum, de distribucionibus diuidendis inter canonicos residenciarios fiendis, continget, vna cum ceteris eiusdem ecclesie canonicis residenciarijs tociens quociens casus emerserit, proporcionaliter contribuat et contribuere teneatur tantoque de distribucionibus et diuidendis, huiusmodi in premissis, et eorum occasione, statutis temporibus careat, quanto carebit in simili alius eiusdem ecclesie canonicus residenciarius quiscunque.

struck out.

[1] ‘fungatur’ *corrected.*

2 = *D.* 2. ITEM ORDINAMUS, LAUDAMUS, arbitramur, precipimus et declaramus, quod nullo modo liceat preposito capituli ecclesie predicte, nec eciam ipsi capitulo, pecunias illas cum et de quibus ipsius ecclesie vicarijs, et cantariarum ibidem capellanis, alijsque eiusdem ecclesie ministris, vt pro eorum salarijs, vel salariorum suorum nomine, debeat

and dedicated; as judge, umpire, giver of the award, and friendly disposer of differences, and as Ordinary and Bishop of the parties and place, in virtue of and by the express terms of the composition aforesaid, and by every means and right by which best we can, following the path of judge, giver of an award, and of a friendly disposer of differences, do bid, decide, award, determine, adjudge, enjoin or ordain, lay down and make pronouncement:

D[1]. 1.
1. Any Dean who is Canon and Prebendary as well as Dean, to benefit and be liable not only as Dean, but also as Canon and Prebendary.

First that since the Dean of the said Church, being a Canon and Prebendary in it, discharges two offices, namely that of Dean, and that of Canon and Prebendary; the aforesaid Mr John the present Dean who is a Canon and Prebendary in the same Church and any future Dean who is Canon and Prebendary in the same Church, and all other Canons of the said Church who are resident Prebendaries, in all causes, pleas, matters and complaints which are raised or shall be raised on behalf of the Chapter, or against the Chapter itself, concerning the proportion which shall affect the Dean himself as Canon and Prebendary and not as Dean in the matter of payments and dividends to be made among the Residentiary Canons; let him contribute and be required to contribute in the same proportion as the rest of the Canons Residentiary of the same Church as often as occasion require, and let him be liable in the matter of these payments and dividends above referred to in exactly the same proportion as in like case any other Residentiary Canon of the same Church shall be liable.

D. 2.
2. The Dean and Chapter to pay in full the Vicars and other inferior Ministers out of the funds existing for this purpose, and not to divert

Also we ordain, decree, decide, order and proclaim that under no circumstances be it lawful for the Provost of the Chapter of the aforesaid Church, nor indeed for the Chapter itself, to spend and use those moneys with and out of which should be paid the Vicars of this Church and the Chantry Chaplains of the same, and other ministers of the same Church (as being for their salaries or on behalf of

[1] 'D' followed by a numeral refers to the section so numbered among the Dean's complaints against the Canons. 'C' followed by a numeral refers in like manner to one of the Canons' complaints against the Dean.

satisfieri; in voluntarijs et quibusvis alijs negocijs seu placitis eciam si Decanus pro tempore existens ad hoc consenciat expendere vel consumere, seu alias disponere de eisdem. Ymo quod primo et ante omnia predictis Vicarijs, Capellanis cantariarum, et ministris huiusmodi, de ipsis pecunijs ut pro suis salarijs, iuxta disposicionem donancium, integre satisfiat, ceteraque onera debita, consueta, et requisita supportentur; et post hec quod superest, inter canonicos residenciarios diuidatur vel in alios ecclesie et Capituli vsus; iuxta ordinaciones super inde factas, disponatur.

3 = D. 3. * Lf. 8b. Concessiones fiant sub nomine decani et capituli.

ITEM ORDINAMUS, LAUDAMUS, arbitramur, precipimus, *declaramus et diffinimus, quod quandocunque Decanus absens fuerit ab ecclesia, liceat Capitulo sub nomine Decani et Capituli *ipsius tamen Decani nomine aut cognomine non expresso* personis bene meritis, pensiones, feoda, annuitates pro obsequijs ipsis ecclesie et Capitulo impensis et impendendis, ad certos annos, vel ad terminum vite sue (nullatenus in perpetuum, nec in feodo) de bonis communibus Capituli que a bonis Decani discreta sunt de consuetudine, vel aliter concedere, ac similes concessiones ratificare et confirmare.

4 = D. 4. De autoritate capituli in dispensacionibus in causis leuibus absente decano.

DECLARAMUS INSUPER, LAUDAMUS, arbitramur et diffinimus, quod Decano presente, sed interesse nolente, aut ipso extra Ecclesiam et Ciuitatem absente, liceat Capitulo super leuibus et minoribus dum tamen ob vtilitatem euidentem, aut necessitatem ecclesie vrgentem cum cause cognicione, sed nullatenus in grauibus vel arduis, in quibus auctoritas vel consensus Episcopi requiritur statuere

their salaries), in unauthorised litigation[1] or any other businesses or pleas, or to dispose of the same money in any other way, even though the Dean for the time being be agreeable to this. Yea because first and before all things the said Vicars, Chantry Chaplains, and such like ministers should be paid in full out of these moneys, as being the provision for their salaries, according to the purpose of those who gave them; and other due, accustomed and necessary charges should be borne; and after this let any surplus be distributed among the Residentiary Canons, or be disbursed for other uses of Church and Chapter; in accordance with the disposition made on this behalf.

these funds or any part of them to any other use, until such ministers have been paid their full salaries.

D. 3.

3. In the absence of the Dean the Chapter may act in the name of Dean and Chapter in the disposition of their own property as distinguished from that of the Dean, so long as they do not make him personally responsible for their acts.

Also we ordain, decree, decide, order, proclaim and determine that whenever the Dean be absent from the Church, it be lawful for the Chapter acting in the name of the Dean and Chapter (so that the Christian and surname of the Dean himself be not used) to grant to fit persons pensions, fees or annuities for services performed or to be performed to the Church and Chapter, for certain periods of years or for life (under no circumstances in perpetuity or in fee) out of the common property of the Chapter as distinct from the property of the Dean, in accordance with custom or otherwise, and to ratify and confirm such grants.

D. 4.

4. The Chapter may decide unimportant matters in the Dean's absence, so long as such decisions be in accordance with statutes and custom.

We proclaim moreover, decree, decide and determine that if the Dean be present but unwilling to take part[2], or if he be away from the Church and city, it be lawful for the Chapter to decide and dispose of slight and unimportant matters, when the convenience of so doing is manifest or the need of the Church pressing, after duly weighing the case; but under no circumstances of matters which are difficult or important in which the authority and consent of the Bishop is necessary; and for them to

[1] The Bishop is here referring to the second of the Dean's complaints (see p. 85) and uses his own words 'in voluntariis.' The expression apparently refers to wilful, vexatious, irresponsible, wasteful litigation, the outcome of the capitular quarrellings.

[2] i.e. if he be in the precincts, but not at the Chapter.

et ordinare; et in ijs que sic statuunt et ordinant dummodo statum ecclesie non concernant Decano presente et non contempto, aut absente, rite, vbi subest iusta causa, dispensare · etiam super statuto iurato: dum tamen contentum in statuto iuratum specialiter non existat.

5=*D*. 5. Hic possit haberi aliquis a forciori pro episcopo vt possit et debeat habere capellanos suos in habitu canonicali sibi assistere et omnino sint ad onus Episcopi et non capituli.

SIMILITER ORDINAMUS et declaramus quod quilibet canonicus residenciarius dicte ecclesie nostre habeat Capellanum aut Clericum, suis sumptibus ad ipsum in habitu chori in ingressu Chori et Capituli, ac egressu sequendum, et sibi in diuinis in dictis ecclesia et Capitulo obsequendum. Nolumus tamen quod ad huiusmodi obsequium aliquem chori vicarium, capellanum, vel clericum habitum chori gerentem, et ad interessendum horis canonicis aut magne misse, seu processionibus, statuto ordinacione seu consuetudine constrictum, eo in tempore quo sic interesse tenetur, euocet vel retrahat · nec eciam quemcunque de habitu ad sic diuinis interessendum obligatum, secum in suis obsequijs vel negocijs extra ciuitatem educat. ['Vide registrum novum pag. 28.' *P*.]

6=*D*. 6. ITEM ORDINAMUS, declaramus, laudamus, arbitramur et diffinimus, ut vacantibus cantariis, quarum collacio vel presentacio ad Decanum et capitulum, vel solum ad Capitulum pertinet · ipsas cantarias cum de earum vacacione certitudinaliter constet, dicti Decanus et Capitulum, aut Capitulum ipsum, personis idoneis infra quadraginta dies a tempore note vacacionis, ad omne minus si breuius tempus pro collacione vel presentacione huiusmodi in ipsarum cantariarum ordinacione statutum non existat conferant vel conferat, personasve huiusmodi presentent vel presentet ad easdem. Alioquin hijs quibus collacio
* Lf. 9[a]. vel presentacio huiusmodi per nec*ligenciam ipsius Capituli deuoluta existat, deuolucionem illam infra quindecim dies extunc immediate sequentes si breuius tempus ad hoc non sit assignatum intimare omnino Capitulum teneatur.

grant dispensation duly where there is good reason in these cases which they so decide and dispose of (so long as they do not concern the establishment of the Church) whether the Dean be present (but not in defiance of him) or whether he be away; even though it be about a statute which they have sworn to, provided only that the matter contained in the statute have not been the subject of a special oath.

D. 5.
5. Canons to maintain their chaplains at their own cost, and not to take away on any business clerks with special duties at times when they are due to perform such duties.

Likewise we ordain and proclaim that every residentiary Canon of our said Church maintain his chaplain or clerk at his own costs to follow him in choir habit at the entering of the choir and Chapter and at the leaving thereof, and to serve him in divine service in the said Church or Chapter. It is not our will however that any call away or keep back for such service any vicar of the choir, chaplain or clerk who wears the choir habit and who is bound by statute, ordinance or custom to take part in the Canonical hours, High Mass or processions, at that time when he is due so to take his part. Nor indeed may any [Canon] take away with him as engaged in his own service or business outside the city any member of the body[1] so bound to take part in divine service.

D. 6.
6. Vacant chantries to be filled by the Chapter within 40 days of such vacancy.

Also we ordain, proclaim, decree, decide and determine that when chantries become void, the collation or presentation to which belongs to the Dean and Chapter, or to the Chapter alone; the said Dean and Chapter, or the Chapter alone, shall bestow these chantries on suitable persons, or present such persons to the same, when the fact of their avoidance is ascertained with certainty, within 40 days from the date of their ascertained avoidance, unless indeed a shorter period be fixed for such collation and presentation in the ordinance governing these chantries. Otherwise let the Chapter be bound to inform those on whom such collation and presentation devolves through the negligence of the Chapter itself, of the fact of this devolving, within 15 days immediately following (if a shorter time be not fixed for this purpose).

[1] '*Quemcumque de habitu,*' i.e. any vicar, chaplain or clerk who is bound to wear the choir habit—or is, as we say, 'of the *cloth.*'

7=*D.* 7, 8. (Here the Bp combines two of the Dean's complaints under one article.) Nota de auctoritate Episcopi quatenus usus legatorum.

ITEM ORDINAMUS, laudamus, arbitramur et diffinimus, vt bona quecunque vna cum certo onere ad certum et determinatum vsum in dicta ecclesia nostra ex pia fidelium deuocione donata, legata vel largita, ad illum si ad onera imposita sufficiant et non alium vsum absque auctoritate sedis apostolice conuertantur. et si ad vsum determinatum non sufficiant, aut conuerti non possunt, in alios pios vsus, absque auctoritate Episcopi nullatenus conuertantur. Alia vero bona non cum certo onere simili modo donata, sub vsu in donacione determinato remaneant; et nullatenus in alium conuertantur sicuti penas a iure in hac parte inflictas in premissis delinquentes voluerint euitare.

8=*D.* 9.

ITEM LAUDAMUS, arbitramur et diffinimus, quod singuli canonici ecclesie nostre Lincolñ residenciarij pannum pro pauperibus clericis vestiendis, eis per Capitulum liberatum, in eosdem, et nullatenus in alios vel alienos, nececiam in proprios ipsorum canonicorum, vsus conuertant et disponant. Alioquin si contrarium fecerit aliquis eorundem, duplum tanti panni in quantitate et valore suis proprijs expensis et sumptibus prouidere, et in vsus eorundem pauperum, et non in alios, disponere teneatur quilibet canonicus in premissis delinquens.

9=*D.* 10; cf. p. 194.

ITEM CUM SECUNDUM antiquam et laudabilem ecclesie nostre predicte obseruatam consuetudinem, quam in hac parte approbamus, nullus canonicus eiusdem ecclesie residenciarius ad faciendum inibi residenciam minorem, nisi prius ibidem in maiori steterit residencia, et eam per triennium continuam compleuerit, admittatur; laudamus, arbitramur et diffinimus, nullum ad faciendum minorem residenciam, nisi prius maiorem fecerit in forma predicta, admitti debere, nisi Capitulum ex necessaria causa et ad vtilitatem ecclesie, super hoc duxerit aliter dispensandum.

Nota de minori residencia.

10=*D.* 11; *C.* 24, 25. De inspeccione munimentorum.

ITEM ORDINAMUS, decernimus, laudamus, arbitramur et diffinimus, ut Decanus dicte Ecclesie nostre Lincolñ

D. 7, 8. 7. Legacies to be devoted to the object for which they were given, and not to be put to any other use.

Also we ordain, decree, decide and determine that all property which has been given, left or bestowed by the pious devotion of the faithful with a definite obligation for a definite use in our said Church be devoted to that use (if it be sufficient for the proper obligation) and to no other, without the authority of the apostolic see; and if it be not sufficient and cannot be devoted to the use prescribed let it under no circumstances be turned to other pious uses without the authority of the Bishop. But let other property, which has not been given in like manner with a definite obligation, remain in use as prescribed in the donation; and let it under no circumstances be turned to any other object, as those who are remiss in the foregoing directions wish to escape the penalties legally inflicted in such case.

D. 9. 8. Cloth provided for the vesting of poor clerks to be used for this purpose and no other.

Also we decree, decide and determine that all Canons Residentiary of our Church of Lincoln use and expend the cloth delivered to them by the Chapter for the vesting of Poor Clerks, on the same, and under no circumstances on others or strangers, nor again for the personal benefit of the Canons themselves. Else if any of the same do otherwise, let any Canon guilty in the aforesaid matter be bound to provide double the quantity of such cloth both in value and measurement at his own cost and charges, and for the use of the same Poor Clerks and no others.

D. 10. 9. No Canons to be permitted to protest lesser residence unless they have kept greater residence for three consecutive years, or have special permission given.

Also since according to the ancient and praiseworthy custom observed in our aforesaid Church, of which in this point we approve, no Residentiary Canon of the said Church is allowed to keep shorter residence in it unless he has first lived there in greater residence and has kept it consecutively for three years, we decree, decide and determine that no one should be permitted to keep shorter residence unless he has first kept the longer in the manner aforesaid unless the Chapter think for some necessary reason and for the benefit of the Church that it may be otherwise allowed in this point.

D. 11. 10. The Dean to

Also we ordain, resolve, decree, decide and determine that every Dean of our said Church of Lincoln have free

quiscunque liberum ad thesaurariam ecclesie, et locum alium quemcunque repositorium, [vbi] munimenta acta et evidencie communia Ecclesie reponuntur, ad illa scrutanda et videnda habeat ingressum; associatis sibi ad hoc per Capitulum duobus Canonicis de Capitulo assignatis, qui secum vt omnis suspicio tollatur in huiusmodi scrutinio personaliter intersint.

[*non habet* MS.]

11 = *D.* 12. Nota de tempore vac[acionis sedis]. * Lf. 9[b].

ITEM ORDINAMUS, decernimus, laudamus, arbitramur et diffinimus, *quod cum vigore cuiusdam ordinacionis in ea parte habite, in singulis vacacionibus sedis episcopalis Lincolñ duo sunt iudices ordinarij, vterque [in locis] sibi limitatis, videlicet, officialis Lincolñ, et Decanus ecclesie nostre, nullus eorum in alterum, pro exercicio iurisdiccionis episcopalis aut locis causisve seu negocijs alterius dicioni per ordinacionem predictam subiectis et attributis, iurisdiccionem exerceat Episcopalem, cum par in parem imperium non habeat, aut potestatem: Nec quis falcem suam mittere debeat in messem alienam.

12 = *D.* 13. Quando operabitur contradiccio decani.

ITEM ORDINAMUS, LAUDAMUS, arbitramur et diffinimus, quod liceat Capitulo temporibus futuris in causis et negocijs communam ecclesie et residenciariorum concernentibus intentandis vel defendendis, cum bona Decani et Capituli in ea parte sint discreta, attornatos in curijs regis, aut alia seculari, sub nomine Decani et Capituli deputare et constituere (cuius Decani contradiccionem, si presens sit/ nisi quod in contrarium racionabile ostendat/ seu absenciam premissis volumus non obesse) poteritque insuper Capitulum, si hoc elegerit, (Decano huiusmodi attornatorum constitucionibus dissenciente, vel reclamante sine causa) Episcopo ad hoc conqueri, qui ipsum Decanum ad hoc vel aliud ad quod tenetur compellere debet et artare.

13 = *D.* 14. De reparacione hospiciorum canonicalium infra clausum.

ITEM ORDINAMUS, decernimus, laudamus, arbitramur et diffinimus, quod annis singulis perpetuis futuris temporibus Decanus et Cancellarius Ecclesie nostre Lincolñ, aut, Decano absente, Precentor et Cancellarius, seu ipso

right of entry to the treasury of the Church and to all other chambers where are laid up the common muniments, acts and evidences of the Church, to examine and view them; two Canons chosen out of the Chapter being associated with him for this purpose by the Chapter to take part personally with him in all such examination, that all suspicion may be removed.

have two Canons associated with him for the inspection of the muniments.

Also we ordain, resolve, decree, decide and determine that, since by force of a certain ordinance dealing with the event, in every vacancy of the see of Lincoln there are two 'iudices ordinarii' each within his own limits, namely the Official of Lincoln and the Dean of our Church, neither of them exercise episcopal jurisdiction against the other, in the exercise of episcopal jurisdiction in places or cases or businesses which are subject and belonging to the province of the other by the aforesaid ordinance, since equal has not power or authority over equal; nor should anyone thrust his sickle into another man's crop.

11. In cases of vacancy in the See of Lincoln each of the 'iudices ordinarii' to confine himself to his own sphere.

And we ordain, decree, decide and determine that it be lawful for the Chapter in future in causes and businesses affecting the interests[1] of the Church and residentiaries which have to be investigated or defended, since the property of the Dean and Chapter in this event is separate, to commission and appoint attorneys in the King's Court or any other secular court, in the name of the Dean and Chapter, and we will that the opposition of the Dean, if he be present, unless he show reasonable cause to the contrary, or his absence be no obstacle to the foregoing procedure; and moreover that the Chapter, if it decide on this course, if the Dean disagree to this appointing of attorneys and protest against it without due cause, shall be able to complain to the Bishop in this matter, and he shall force and compel the Dean himself to this or any other course of action to which he is canonically bound.

D. 13.
12. The Chapter may appoint attorneys in the civil courts to look after their interests, and if the Dean oppose them may appeal to the Bishop to compel him to act with them.

Also we ordain, resolve, decree, decide and determine that every year perpetually for the future the Dean and Chancellor of our Church of Lincoln, or if the Dean be away the Precentor and Chancellor, or if the Precentor

D. 14.
13. A committee of three to inspect Canons'

[1] *or* 'common fund.'

Nota ordinem deputacionis duos de capitulo in casu hic expresso et utrum is... habetur et in vigore imperpetuum singulos annos.

Precentore aut Cancellario absente eorum alter presens et Subdecanus, infra vnum mensem post festum Purificacionis beate Marie virginis, incipiendo ad festum Purificacionis beate Marie iam proxime futurum, videant personaliter assumpto sibi clerico camere communis omnia et singula mansiones siue hospicia canonicalia infra clausum dicte ecclesie existencia: et canonicos ipsa hospicia inhabitantes moneant ut defectus in ipsis hospicijs per visum huiusmodi repertos, et reparacione indigentes, infra medietatem anni proxime sequentis competenter reparent pro vt decet. quodque ipsi Canonici reparaciones huiusmodi infra quindenam post festum Sancti Michaelis extunc proxime futuri simili modo superuideant, et si reperirint huiusmodi monitos competentem defectuum repertorum non fecisse reparacionem; extunc in proxima diuisione inter canonicos fienda tantum de porcione non reparantis subtrahatur, quantum sufficere possit ad congruam reparacionem defectuum non reparatorum et hoc substractum in reparacionibus defectuum huiusmodi in proximo anno per ipsum Capitulum disponatur. Consimiliter inquiri et

* Lf. 10ª. videri ac moniciones *Capitulo fieri volumus, quo ad similia hospicia canonicalia in manibus capituli infra dictum clausum existencia seu ad eius vel fabrice ecclesie reparacionem spectancia sub pena interdicti in ipsum Capitulum, si in premissis reparacionibus negligens fuerit vel remissum, per nos et successores nostros fulminandi.

14. ['Dividentia unde oritur.' *P.*]

ITEM ORDINAMUS, laudamus, &c., quod ante diuisionem inter Canonicos de fructibus et prouentibus ac bonis ad communam pertinentibus fiendam, primo et ante omnia soluantur stipendia ministrorum dicte Ecclesie officiancium et deseruiencium, distribuciones quotidiane, vina, obitus;

himself or Chancellor be away, then either of them who is on the spot and the sub-dean, within one month after the Feast of the Purification of the Blessed Virgin Mary, beginning with the Feast of the Purification of Blessed Mary now next occurring, view in person (taking with them the clerk of the Common Chamber) all and each of the Canons' residences or dwelling-houses existing within the Close of the said Church, and warn the Canons inhabiting these dwelling-houses to make good properly, as is fit, the defects found in these houses at the inspection and which need repair, within the first six months of the year following[1]; and that these Canons view in like manner such repairs within 15 days after the Feast of St Michael next occurring, and if they find that those warned in this matter have not put into proper repair the defects which were found, then in the next distribution that is to be made among the Canons, so much shall be deducted from the share of him who has not done his repairs as shall suffice for the due repair of the defects which have not been put right, and that this sum deducted be expended in this setting right of defects in the following year by the Chapter itself. And in like manner we will that there be examination and inspection made and warning given to the Chapter in the case of like canonical dwellings which are in the hands of the Chapter and are situate within the said Close which pertain to the repair of the same or of the fabric of the Church; under pain of interdict to be launched by us or our successors against the Chapter itself if it be negligent or remiss in the matter of repairs above dealt with.

residences in the close and to order repairs to be made good.

Also we ordain, decree etc. that before division be made among the Canons of the fruits, rents and goods belonging to the common fund, first and before all there be paid the stipends of the ministers who officiate in and serve the said Church, (and) the daily distributions, wines, and obits;

14. The stipends and allowances of the ministers to be the first charge on the income of the Church.

[1] i.e. before September 29—St Michael's Day. The Purification falls on Feb. 2, and the year began on March 25. Holy Rood Day, the annual audit at Lincoln, occurs on Sept. 14, a fortnight before Michaelmas.

deductisque alijs oneribus ecclesie incumbentibus, *quod superest inter Canonicos diuidatur.*

15. Nota quod pro Capitulo fideciarij sunt ii : sufficiant duo.

ITEM ARBITRAMUR, laudamus, &c., quod cum nos aut aliquis Successorum nostrorum Episcoporum Ecclesie Lincolñ post visitacionem nostram et suam in eadem exercitam Decano et capitulo detecta in nostra aut sua visitacione miserimus aut miserit corrigenda ad huiusmodi correccionem faciendam conuocentur pro Capitulo per Decanum, aut alium Capituli presidentem, omnes Canonici residentes et presentes · in cuius Capituli locum duos canonicos per Decanum et Capitulum iuxta tenorem Laudi in ea parte lati assumptos, non posse succedere, vel loco Capituli sufficere declaramus et arbitramur cum super hoc inter Decanum et Capitulum, veluti de re certa et indubitata, per sententiam diffinitiuam declarata, vt in compromissum veniret, non fuerit dictum aut cogitatum.

Et nota de Presidenti in absencia decani.

16. Nota nullo modo [dis]pensari vt stans [in ob]sequio alterius percip[iat cum] aliis residenciari[js].

ITEM ARBITRAMUR, &c., dispensaciones per Decanum et capitulum, seu presidentem et capitulum, de cetero fiendas, vt aliquis canonicus residenciarius in maiori vel minori, in aliqua curia spirituali aut temporali, aut alicuius domini spiritualis aut temporalis obsequio, ad certum quotum numerum annorum, insistat extra ecclesiam, et nichilominus pro residenciario habeatur, ac distribuciones quotidianas communasve aut obitus, et vina, seu alia iura residencialia percipiat, ac si in ecclesia resideret personaliter, improbamus et cassamus, ac eas, cum sine diminucione cultus diuini, ac ecclesie nostre depressione, concedi vel recipi non possint, improbas, nullas et inualidas fore declaramus. et tam illum qui imposterum talem dispensacionem obtinuerit, aut ea vsus fuerit, ⟨quam⟩ singulares personas sic capitulariter dispensantes, maioris excommunicacionis sentenciam incurrere volumus ipso facto: per hoc non intendentes ipsum a pena exuere qua presens nostrum laudum quo ad premissa et subsequencia intendimus roborare.

and after other charges imposed upon the Church have been allowed for, let what remains over be divided among the Canons.

15. In the case of settling points noted for correction by the Bishop at his visitation, the whole Chapter to act, and not two deputies only on their behalf.

Also we decide, decree etc. that when we or any of our successors the Bishops of the Church of Lincoln after our and their visitations held in the same Church remit a list of matters noted for correction, all the resident and present Canons be gathered together as representing the Chapter for such correction through the Dean or other President of the Chapter. And we proclaim and order that the two Canons chosen by the Dean and Chapter in accordance with the tenor of the award put forth in that case, to act for the Chapter, cannot take the place of or act on behalf of the Chapter, since it was neither proposed nor supposed that this point should enter into the terms of composition between the Dean and the Chapter, as though it were a plain and unambiguous matter and the subject of a definitive pronouncement.

16. No dispensations to be granted to Canons in full enjoyment of their rights to follow another career, under pain of excommunication.

Also we decide etc. that we condemn and annul the giving of dispensations for the future by the Dean and Chapter or President and Chapter to any Residentiary Canon, whether in greater or in lesser residence, to be engaged away from the Church in any spiritual or temporal court, or in the service of any spiritual or temporal lord for any fixed term of years, and none the less to be regarded as a Residentiary and to be in receipt of the daily distributions or commons, or obits and wines or other rights of a Residentiary as if he were in personal residence at the Church; and we declare that these dispensations (since they cannot be granted or received without the lessening the dignity of Divine Service and the lowering of the tone of our Church) shall be bad, null and void. And we will that he who for the future shall obtain such dispensation or shall use it, and all persons granting such dispensations by virtue of their capitular authority, incur *ipso facto* the sentence of greater excommunication; not intending hereby to exempt him from the penalty[1] by means of which we purpose to fortify this award of ours both as regards what has already gone before and what follows.

[1] See p. 141 below.

17. De Inventorijs [tri]plicatis conscr[ibendis, et a] quibus conseruant[ur]. * Lf. 10b.

ITEM CUM A NONNULLIS nobis sit relatum quod bona ecclesie nostre Lincolñ, *vtpote calices, vestimenta, libri, aliaque iocalia, et vasa tam aurea quam argentea eciam deaurata, aliaque nonnulla supellectilia et implementa que sub cura et custodia Thesaurarij dicte Ecclesie pro tempore existentis debent remanere multum segniter et indiscrete nimis conseruantur; propter quod de eorum subtraccione vel alienacione timeatur; petitumque a nobis inter cetera in compromissis predictis contenta, vt Dominum Johannem Leek Sacristam dicte ecclesie nostre qui custodie bonorum huiusmodi sub dicto thesaurario, vt eius minister, intendit, ad compotum siue raciocinium reddendum, et fidele iuramentum conficiendum, de bonis eisdem compellamus: Nos igitur aduertentes onus et curam huiusmodi thesaurario pro tempore existenti, et non Sacriste incumbere; laudamus, ordinamus, decernimus, arbitramur, precipimusque et diffinimus, quod Thesaurarius dicte ecclesie qui nunc est circa festum Sancti Michaelis Archangeli proxime iam futurum coram aliquibus probis et discrecioribus Capituli eiusdem ecclesie nostre, de omnibus et singulis bonis dicte ecclesie nostre ad curam et custodiam ipsius Thesaurarij spectantibus, in quibuscunque rebus seu corporibus consistant, fieri faciat inuentaria plena et fidelia, seu Regestra consimilia triplicata in quibus scribatur in quo statu officium huiusmodi recepit; et quot que et qualia iam inibi extent calices, libri, vestimenta, ornamenta, supellectilia, iocalia, vasa aurea et argentea, et similia, in quibuscunque rebus consistant. quodque inuentaria seu Regestra huiusmodi clare et integre infra quindenam post festum sancti Michaelis quolibet anno semel in presencia capituli, vel electorum per Capitulum, in aliquo congruo, visui supponantur. quodque in eisdem inuentarijs seu Regestris, omnia et singula similia bona iocalia que ipsi ecclesie nostre in vita dicti Thesaurarij ex largicione nobilium, seu deuo-

17. The treasurer to keep henceforth three inventories or registers of the ornaments etc. of the Church, to be checked once a year and to be kept one in his own charge, the second in the common chest, and the third by the Bishop.

And since we have been informed by several persons that property of our Church of Lincoln, such as chalices, vestments, books and other treasures[1] and vessels of gold and silver and silver-gilt and certain other furniture and ornaments (which should remain in the care and custody of the Treasurer for the time being of the said Church), are kept very laxly and too carelessly, on which account there is some fear of their loss and alienation, and since we have been asked among other things contained in the aforesaid composition to compel Mr John Leeke the Sacrist[2] of our said Church (who looked after the safe custody of such goods under the said Treasurer as his assistant) to render an account or return and to take a strict oath as regards these same goods; we therefore holding that a burden or responsibility of this kind should rest upon the Treasurer for the time being and not on the Sacrist, decree, ordain, resolve, decide, command and determine that the Treasurer of the said Church who now is[3], about the feast of St Michael the Archangel now next occurring, in the presence of any honest and discreet members of the Chapter of our same Church, cause to be made full and faithful inventories or registers, three in number and exactly corresponding, of all and singular the goods of our said Church which come under the care and custody of the Treasurer himself of whatsoever kind or nature they consist; and that in them it be noted in what condition he took over this office; and how many, what, and of what kind there now belong to it chalices, books, vestments, ornaments, furniture, treasures, vessels of gold and silver and such like, of whatsoever nature they consist. And that such inventories or registers clearly and completely be subjected to inspection once in each year within 15 days after the Feast of St Michael, in the presence of the Chapter or representatives of the Chapter, in some convenient place. And that in the same inventories or registers the same Treasurer shall cause likewise to be written down all and singular the goods and treasures

[1] jocalia: jewels. For specimens of Lincoln Cathedral Inventories see *Archaelogia* vol. LIII. (1892).

[2] J. Leeke the Sacristan was also Rector of Broxholme. Some very serious accusations were brought against him at the Bishop's Visitation in 1437, but apparently without being proved.

[3] John Haget was treasurer 1406–1442.

cione fidelium concedente Domino donari vel legari continget, similiter inscribi faciet idem Thesaurarius; quorum inuentariorum sive Regestrorum vnum ponatur et seruetur in archa communi: vbi Sigillum commune est solitum custodiri, seu loco alio congruenti · et aliud maneat penes ipsum Thesaurarium, futuro Thesaurario successori suo reseruandum; Tercium quoque penes nos et successores nostros Episcopos Lincolñ futuros in nostri et suo officio Regestrum remaneat conseruandum. quodque quilibet futurus Thesaurarius infra vnum mensem post induccionem et installacionem suas, similia inuentaria siue Regestra modo et forma simili fieri faciat: et eorum vnum liberet in dicta archa conseruandum; et aliud penes se retineat, suo successori vt premissum est reseruandum;
* Lf. 11a. Et *tercium nobis vel successoribus nostris Episcopis Lincolñ, penes nos et ipsos successores nostros liberet conseruandum.

18=C.1.2. Nota quod decanus debet pascere certis festis siue sit presens siue [non].

ITEM CUM PROBACIONES super infra memorato articulo coram nobis producte et ministrate obscure et ambigue existant nec pro vna aut alia parte sufficienter concludentes quia *tamen* ex antiquis scripturis in manibus cancellarij ecclesie nostre racione officij sui repertis, nonnullos Decanos absentes inuenimus pastuum onera in principalibus festis, eciam absentes, agnouisse et subijsse · Decanusque quiscunque pro tempore existens ad faciendum in dicta ecclesia residenciam debitam et consuetam videlicet per triginta et quatuor septimanas et quinque dies in anno quolibet, secundum ipsius ecclesie consuetudinem, quam approbamus et sic de cetero in dicta ecclesia obseruandam fore declaramus, iuramento suo astringatur: et iuxta librum consuetudinarium festis ipsis principalibus duplicibus in odem libro expressatis, absente Episcopo, Regumque et Episcoporum obitibus diuinum exequi officium teneatur; confessusque sit prefatus Magister Johannes Decanus modernus, se presentem Episcopo absente et celebrare et pascere velle, et sic pre-

per triginta [iiij.] septimanas et [.v. dies].

[*Liber Niger*, p.281.] (The marginal numerals preceded by the

which shall happen to be bestowed on or left to this Church of ours during the lifetime of the said Treasurer by the liberality of the nobility or the devotion of the faithful, through the favour of the Lord; and that of these inventories or registers, one be placed and preserved in the common chest where the common seal is wont to be kept, or in some other suitable place; and a second remain in the possession of the Treasurer himself to be kept for the next Treasurer who succeeds him; and that the third register remain to be preserved in charge of us and our successors the future Bishops of Lincoln in our and their official registry. And that every future Treasurer within one month of his induction and installation cause to be made like inventories and registers of like kind and arrangement, and that he deliver one of them to be kept in the said chest; and retain a second in his own custody to be preserved for his successor as has been said above; and deliver the third to us and our successors the Bishops of Lincoln to be preserved in our charge and that of our successors.

C. 1. 2. 18. **The Dean to feed the choir on all Principal Doubles and other Feasts if the Bishop is away.**

Also since the evidences produced and laid before us as to the article dealt with below are doubtful and ambiguous, nor sufficiently conclusive on the one side or the other; since nevertheless we find from ancient documents discovered in the possession of the Chancellor of our Church by virtue of his office, that several Deans though absent have recognised and submitted to the burden of feeding the choir on the principal feasts despite their absence; and each Dean for the time being is bound by his oath to keep his due and accustomed residence in the same Church, namely 34 weeks and 5 days in each year, according to the custom of this Church, which we approve and order so to be observed henceforward in the same Church; and according to the Consuetudinary on those Feasts which are principal doubles and are mentioned by name in the same book, if the Bishop be away, and at the obits of Kings and Bishops, he is required to perform the divine office; and the aforesaid Mr John the present Dean has avowed that he is willing to be present, if the Bishop be away

initial ‘*C*’ are inserted for the sake of reference to the complaints of the Canons, pp. 56—70; ‘*D*’, those of Dean Macworth, are on pp. 84—90.)

sentem celebrasse et pauisse: alijque habentes in dicta ecclesia nostra dignitates, quarum pretextu certis festis tenentur celebrare, festis ipsis ministros chori eciam pascere, licet absentes, hactenus consueuerint; et sic pascant pacifice, et sine contradiccione, Nos in consciencia nostra tuciorem viam eligentes, ad honorem Dei, et [eius] gloriose Dei genitricis, ecclesie predicte vtilitatem, vberius-que confortamen ministrorum eiusdem, qui die et nocte in horis diurnis et nocturnis psallendo, legendo, alijsque multipliciter diuinis obsequijs sedule intendendo, portant pondus diei et estus, vt eo hijs liberius insistant, quo vt in releuamine diminucionis prouentuum suorum qui hijs diebus multo decreuerunt, senserunt se refectos; laudamus, arbitramur, &c., dictum Magistrum Johannem Decanum

[‘Decanus debet pascere eciam absens.’ *P*.]

modernum, et quemlibet eius successorem dicte ecclesie nostre Lincolñ Decanum post eum futurum, tam absentem quam presentem, ad pascendum chorum siue ministros chori dicte ecclesie nostre Lincolñ in supra memoratis festis, et alijs, prout in ipso libro consuetudinario seriosius exprimuntur, absente Episcopo imperpetuum teneri et compelli debere. Quodque idem Decanus onera que pre-

De ignitegijs.

sens in festis et obitibus predictis circa pulsacionem ignitegiorum noscitur agnouisse, ipse, et successores sui eciam absentes agnoscere et subire teneantur.

19=*C*. 3. De exhibicione Vicarij per decanum.

Item arbitramur, laudamus, &c., quod Decanus modernus ecclesie nostre, et quiscunque eius successor Decanus futurus, prebendam optinens in eadem (dummodo com-

* Lf. 11[b].

petens sit) residenciam non faciens maiorem *vel minorem quamuis resideat ut Decanus ac quiuis alius canonicus eciam competentem obtinens prebendam, vicarium in choro ecclesie nostre ad deseruiendum et officiandum pro eodem in diuinis exhibere et habere, ad soluendum eidem salarium consuetum terminis solitis teneatur, et sic ex-

and officiate and feed the choir, and that he has been so present and has officiated and fed the choir; and others holding dignities in our said Church by virtue of which they are required to officiate on certain Feasts, have been accustomed hitherto, though absent, on those Feasts to feed the ministers of the choir, and so do feed them without gainsaying or controversy; we conscientiously choosing the safer way to the honour of God and of his glorious Mother, to the benefit of the aforesaid Church and the richer comfort of the ministers of the same, who day and night, in the day and night hours, in the singing of psalms, in reading of lessons and by their earnest attention to the many other duties of divine service bear the burden and heat of the day, in order that they may the more freely give their attention to these labours as they have felt themselves refreshed, by way of relief of the diminution of their incomes which in these days have much decreased; we decree and decide etc. that the said Mr John the present Dean, and each successor of his who shall be Dean after him of our said Church of Lincoln, shall be bound and required for ever whether absent or present to feed the choir or the ministers of the choir of our said Church of Lincoln on the above-mentioned Feasts, and on other Feasts as set down more particularly in the Consuetudinary, if the Bishop be away. And that the same Dean and his successors be required to recognise and submit to, even though absent, the burdens connected with the ringing of the curfew[1] on the Feasts and obits aforesaid, which he is known to have recognised [as due from him] when he is present.

C. 3. 19. **The Dean being a Prebendary as well is to be represented by two Vicars, by one as Dean, by the other as Prebendary.**

Also we decide and decree etc. that the present Dean of our Church and each successive future Dean after him who holds a prebend in the same (if it be sufficient) who does not keep either greater or lesser residence (though he be in residence as Dean) and any other Canon who holds a sufficient prebend, be required to have and maintain a Vicar in the choir of our Church to serve and officiate in his place in divine service, and to pay the same the accustomed salary at the accustomed times, and that he

[1] Cf. *L.C.S.* I. (Black Book), pp. 370, 385–6.

hibeat habeat et soluat. Ad que in personam Decani sic arbitrari et laudare ex eo potissime mouemur, quod in persona sua duo concurrere cernimus iura, In quibus ac si in personis duorum essent, idem censemus obser-uandum: prebendam vero ad exhibicionem huiusmodi vicarij competentem reputamus, cuius verus valor ceteris oneribus deductis ad iiij^or libras annuas communibus annis se extendit.

Nota quatuor libras [deducendo] septimas.

20 = *C*. 4. ITEM LICET paris condicionis in lucro et onere esse debent omnes canonici residenciarij ecclesie Lincolñ nostre, et ex racione et iuris disposicione non sit ferendus qui lucrum amplectitur, et onus eidem annexum recusat et a se excutit. quia tamen reperimus ex antiquis registris et euidencijs dicte ecclesie nostre sub fida custodia existentibus, a tanto tempore de quo non extat memoria obseruatum fuisse pacifice et quiete quod Decani ecclesie nostre prebendati residenciam canonicalem in maiori facientes in eadem, quamuis non celebrant in cursu neque pascant, connumerari et concurrere consueuerunt cum alijs Canonicis maiorem eciam residenciam facientibus, *in distribucione septimarum in secundo anno* in quo sic inceperint residere, ac in tercio et sic deinceps. Arbitramur, laudamus, &c., Decanos ecclesie nostre Lincolñ predicte quoscunque pro tempore existentes a celebrando et pascendo in cursu liberos fore et immunes.

[*underlined*]

21 = *C*. 4. ITEM ARBITRAMUR, laudamus, &c., quod Decanus predictus et ceteri sui successores Decani ecclesie nostre futuri in maiori vel in minori residencia existentes, seu postquam sic residere inceperint licet ipsam ex causa necessaria dimiserint et per se aut alios celebrantes in propria et pascentes; a solucione septimarum suarum exonerentur ac liberi sint et quieti, Si vero Decanus pro tempore existens canonicaliter non resederit, nec huius-

[‘Decanus semel in residencia majori pro tempore existens (et postea desistens) non solvet septimas.’ *P*.]

so maintain, have and pay him; and we are the more particularly moved so to order and decree this as regards the person of the Dean, because we see two different jurisdictions vested concurrently in his one person, as to which we think that the same law should be observed as if they were vested in two persons. And we count sufficient for the maintenance of such a vicar, that prebend whereof the actual value after other charges have been deducted amounts to £4 per annum on a yearly average.

C. 4. 20. The Dean as Prebendary to rank with prebendaries in the distribution of septisms. But as Dean to be exempt from these duties.

Also though all the Residentiary Canons of our Church of Lincoln ought to be in the same position both as to their pay and their duties, and in reason and justice he is unpardonable who takes the pay and repudiates and avoids the duties attached to it; since however we find from the old registers and evidences of our Church which have remained in safe keeping that it has been from time immemorial the accepted and agreed practice for the Deans of our Church keeping greater residence in the same as prebendaries (though they neither officiate in course[1] nor feed the choir) to be counted and rank with other Canons who keep greater residence in the distribution of septisms in the second year in which they so began to reside, and in the third and so on; We decide, decree etc. that all Deans for the time being of our aforesaid Church of Lincoln shall be free and excused from officiating and feeding in course.

C. 4. 21. A Dean residing and performing his turn as Prebendary to be excused payment of septisms. Not otherwise.

Also we decide, decree etc. that the aforesaid Dean and other Deans his successors in the future of our Church of Lincoln, being in greater or lesser residence, or after they have begun so to reside (though they have given it up for some necessary cause), and either by themselves or by others officiating in their own turn[2] and feeding; be excused, freed and released from the payment of their septisms. If however the Dean for the time being has not resided

[1] *in cursu*: his week's duty taken by a residentiary Canon in the place of one of the non-residentiary absentees.

[2] *in propria* [*septimana*]: a residentiary Canon's own 'turn' of a week's duty at the Minster, as distinguished from residences 'in course' undertaken for absent prebendaries.

modi residenciam inceperit licet vt Decanus resideat, cum vt Decanus altitate differat a se ipso vt Canonico, a solucione huiusmodi septimarum nullatenus excusetur quamuis ad celebrandum in propria se obtulerit et pascendum.

22 (xxij. MS.) = C. 5. 7. ITEM ARBITRAMUR, laudamus, &c., quod in omnibus et singulis causis et negocijs, quorum cognicio et expedicio ad Decanum pertinet et capitulum ecclesie nostre, Idem Decanus citando. rescribendo. procedendo. diffiniendo. corrigendo, puniendo et cetera exercendo. ea faciat exerceat et expediat nomine suo et capituli, nullatenus sibi ut
* Lf. 12a. proprium *vsurpando quod sibi et capitulo est commune. Ita tamen quod nulla talia aggrediatur agat vel incipiat, nisi deliberacione prehabita cum ipso capitulo, preterquam in casibus sibi specialiter ad contrarium vel aliud faciendum attributis per consuetudinem indubitatam, ordinacionesve aut statuta nostre ecclesie supradicte.

23 = C. 13. Nota in cuius [manibus] debent remanere portarum claves. ITEM ARBITRAMUR, laudamus, &c., quod pro securitate canonicorum ministrorumque ecclesie de nocte surgencium ad matutinas Janitor portarum clausi ecclesie singulis noctibus horis debitis et consuetis claudat portas quarum claues immediate deferat preposito ecclesie nostre, vel ipso absente, sublimiori persone eiusdem ecclesie nostre post Decanum in clauso residenti in cuius manibus resideant per totam illam noctem, Janitori predicto de mane illas petenti retradende. Et si quis Decano aut alicui alteri ecclesie nostre canonico famulancium, Janitorem ipsum sic claudere, clauesque sic portare et tradere, aut ipsum in officij sui huiusmodi debito exercicio turbare vel impedire presumpserit et super hoc conuictus fuerit, dominus suus ipsum a suo obsequio infra tres dies immediate sequentes cum effectu remoueat et expellat;
Nota bene. sub pena quadraginta solidorum in proxima apertura siue distribucione inter canonicos facienda subtrahendorum, et fabrice ecclesie infra tres dies post aperturam siue distribucionem huiusmodi soluendorum.

canonically, nor has begun such residence, though he reside as Dean, since as Dean he occupies a higher position than himself as Canon, let him by no means be released from this payment of septisms although he shall have offered himself to officiate in turn and to feed.

Also we decide and decree etc. that in all and singular causes and businesses of which the cognisance and settlement belong to the Dean and Chapter of our Church, the same Dean do in summoning, deciding, proceeding, judging, correcting, punishing and exercising other powers, so act, exercise power and conclude the matter in the name of himself and the Chapter, by no means arrogating to himself as his own that which belongs to him and the Chapter in common. So nevertheless that he approach, take in hand or enter upon no such matters except after a consultation has been held by him and the Chapter itself, except in cases specially assigñed to him for other or different treatment by undoubted custom or by the ordinances or statutes of our aforesaid Church. C. 5. 22. In all dealing with cases etc. the Dean to act in name of the Chapter as well as in his own, and not in his own name only.

Also we decide, decree etc. that, for the safety of the Canons and ministers of the Church rising at night for Mattins, the gatekeeper of the close of the Church shut the gates every night at the proper and accustomed hours; and that he take their keys at once to the Provost of our Church, or if he be away to that resident in the close who is next highest in rank after the Dean; and that they remain in his hands throughout that whole night and be given back to the aforesaid gatekeeper when he comes for them in the morning. And if any servant of the Dean or of any Canon of our Church shall dare to hinder or disturb the gatekeeper in so locking up and taking and delivering up the keys, or in the due performance of this his office, and shall be convicted of the same, his master shall dismiss him altogether and remove him from his service within the next three days under penalty of forfeiting 40 shillings, at the next making of reckoning and distribution among the Canons, and of paying them towards the fabric of the Church within three days after such reckoning and distribution. C. 13. 23. The gates of the close to be locked at the proper hours at night. Anyone hindering the gatekeeper in his duties to be punished.

24=*C.* 14. ITEM LAUDAMUS, arbitramur, &c., quod Decanus ecclesie nostre quicunque pro tempore existens per se solum iure suo decanali iurisdiccionem in prebendis. locisque aut personis eorundem nullatenus exerceat, cum suum non sit quod in commune cum alijs optinet, sed cum capitulo ecclesie nostre, preterquam in prebendis in Ciuitate nostra Lincolñ, ac alijs in quibus dicti Decanus et Capitulum ad exercendum iurisdiccionem iure vel consuetudine non sunt muniti (causis appellacionum, si que ad ipsum Decanum tantum. absque Capitulo interponi contigerint, ac visitacione sua decanali, correccionibusque detectorum in ipsa[1] sua visitatione. ac ceteris dependentibus ab eadem, nec non hijs que soli Decano presenti per composicionem inter Dominum Bonifacium dudum Archiepiscopum Cantuar' ac Decanum et capitulum ecclesie nostre Lincolñ, pro tempore vacacionis sedis episcopalis eiusdem tribuuntur, duntaxat exceptis).

[1] ['presenti' *P.*]

[A.D. 1261. *Liber Niger*, p. 311.]

25=*C.* 15. ITEM CUM DEDUCTUM et probatum sit coram nobis, quemlibet ecclesie nostre Decanum ad soluendum annuatim clerico communi Capituli viginti et sex solidos et octo denarios ad obitum Domini Wyllielmi Lexington in dicta Ecclesia nostra celebrandum astrictum fore et obligatum; *laudamus, arbitramur, &c., Decanum eiusdem ecclesie nostre modernum et singulos eius successores, ad solucionem prefate summe ad obitum predictum annuatim soluende secundum ordinacionem superinde factam, teneri, et eam absque difficultate soluere debere.

[ob. 8, *al.* 20, Sept. 1272.]

* Lf. 12b.

26=*C.* 17. [Decanus non debet prohibere soluciones capitulo nec recipere redditus.] ITEM ARBITRAMUR laudamus quod non liceat Decano moderno, aut alicui successori suo in ipso decanatu, prohibere aut impedire aliquem debitorem capituli, aut Decani et capituli, ipsi Capitulo, communeve, aut ministris per Capitulum ad hoc deputatis, id soluere ad quod tenetur · cum non intersit Decano condicionem Capituli sic

Also we decree, decide etc. that by no means shall any Dean for the time being of our Church exercise jurisdiction by himself in his own authority as Dean over the prebends, and over places and persons of the same, since that which he holds in conjunction with others is not his own absolutely, but [conjointly] with the Chapter of our Church, except in the case of prebends in our city of Lincoln, and in others in which the said Dean and Chapter are not privileged by law and custom to exercise jurisdiction. With the exception of any causes of appeal which shall be lodged with the Dean himself only and apart from the Chapter; and of his Decanal Visitation and the setting right of things brought to notice in that his Visitation and of other things connected with the same; and with the exception moreover of those powers which were assigned to the present Dean only by the terms of the agreement made between the Lord Boniface late Archbishop of Canterbury and the Dean and Chapter of our Church of Lincoln in the event of a vacancy in the Episcopal See.

C. 14. 24. The Dean to have no jurisdiction over prebends by himself, except in such cases as come under his Visitation powers and certain others.

Also, since it has been proved and made clear before us that every Dean of our Church should be bound and obliged to pay every year to the common clerk of the Chapter twenty six shillings and eight pence for celebrating the obit of the Lord William Lexington in our said Church; we decree and decide etc. that the present Dean of our said Church and each of his successors be held to the payment of the aforesaid sum at the aforesaid obit every year, according to the ordinance already made, and must pay it without making any trouble.

C. 15. 25. The 26/8 to be paid yearly to the common fund at the obit of Bp Lexington.

Also we decide and decree that the present Dean shall not, nor shall any successor of his in the Deanery, prevent or hinder any debtor of the Chapter or of the Dean and Chapter from paying that which is due from him to the Chapter itself, or to the common body, or to the ministers appointed by the Chapter to receive payments. Since the Dean has no business[1] to impoverish the condition of the Chapter by such hindrance; nor yet is he to exact or

C. 17. 26. The Dean not to hinder payment of debts to the Chapter, nor to receive moneys belonging to the Common Body.

[1] Or, 'it is not the Dean's interest' (*non intersit Decano*).

prohibendo facere deteriorem; nec pecunias commune ecclesie debitas eciam a volentibus soluere exigere vel recipere, cum ad hoc non sit per Capitulum deputatus.

27 = *C.* 8. 19. ITEM CUM DE CONSUETUDINE ecclesie nostre temporibus quibus Decanus et capitulum capitulariter debeant conuenire, solus Ecclesie virgarius, absque pluribus, ostium capituli interius stando, clausum solitus est custodire arbitramur, laudamus, &c., quod huiusmodi capitulorum temporibus nullus extraneus, aut canonicorum famulus vel familiaris nisi per Capitulum accersitus, aut vnus solum pro negocio aliquo peragendo per suum dominum euocatus de consensu aut permissu tamen Capituli, incontinenti et absque mora exiturus domum capitularem intrare permittatur Ne per tales astantes et ascultantes Ecclesie secreta in ipsius dampnum ad extra reuelentur seu libertas a canonicis in communicando aut consulendo subtrahatur · aut timor forsan per tales congregatos ibidem incuciendus facta capitularia infringat aut perturbet.

28 = *C.* 21. ['Pulsacio campanarum continuetur vsque adventum executoris officij.'] †ITEM ARBITRAMUR quod vltima pulsacio campanarum ad matutinas primam et vesperas continuetur, et non cesset ante executoris officij aduentum, ad cuiuscunque missum vel mandatum. Nolumus tamen quod executor ille suum aduentum differendo, in tediūm maiorum ecclesie nostre, aut chori ipsius, ipsum prestolando, nimium sit morosus.

29 = *C.* 22. Notatur de missa, de alijs horis. ITEM ARBITRAMUR, &c., quod postquam executor officij magnam missam inchoauerit, non liceat alicui Decano pro tempore existenti ipsum aut chorum, quominus in officio ipso et missa vlterius progrediatur et procedat vllatenus prohibere, seu ipsos ad reincipiendum compellere vel artare.

30 = *C.* 30. ITEM CUM SECUNDUM Ecclesie nostre ritum laudabilem omnes et singuli qui in festis duplicibus et alijs celebrare habeant magnas missas in ecclesia, per vicecancellarium singulis diebus sa*b*ati tabulentur et scribantur. Arbitra-

† Articles 28 and 29 are written in the inverse order in the MS., and then marked '𝔟' and '𝔞' respectively.

receive, even from those willing to pay, moneys due to the common body of the Church, since he is not appointed by the Chapter to act in this capacity.

C. 8. 19. 27. No strangers to be allowed within the Chapter-house at the time of Chapter meetings.

Also, since by a custom of our Church, at those times at which the Dean and Chapter are wont to meet Chapter-wise, the verger of the Church alone without any others has been used, standing himself within, to keep the door of the Chapter-house closed; we decide, decree etc. that at times of Chapter meetings no stranger nor servant or retainer of any of the Canons be permitted to enter the Chapter-house, except he be summoned by the Chapter, or any one be summoned by his master simply to perform some duty (and this with the consent and permission of the Chapter) and shall then depart at once and without delay; lest by such persons standing and listening the private affairs of the Church be made public outside to its detriment; or the Canons be deprived of freedom in speech and deliberation; or the possibility of intimidation being offered by such persons gathering in the same place weaken or confuse the proceedings of the Chapter.

C. 21. 29. The Bells to go on ringing till the arrival of the officiant who is not to be late.

Also we decide that the last ringing of the bells to Mattins, Prime and Evensong be continued and do not cease at a message or order from anyone whatsoever before the arrival of the officiant of the office. Nevertheless we would not have the said officiant be too long in delaying his arrival so as to weary the senior members of our Church, or the choir thereof, in the waiting for him.

C. 22. 28. The Dean not to cause office or Mass to be begun again if he is late.

Also we decide that after the celebrant of the office has begun High Mass no Dean for the time being shall be allowed under any circumstances to prevent him or the choir from going on and proceeding with the office and Mass, nor to force and compel them to begin over again.

C. 30. 30. If the Dean wishes to celebrate on any Feast for

Also since according to the praiseworthy custom of our Church all and each who have to celebrate the High Masses in the Church on Doubles or other Festivals, have their names written out in a table[1] or list every Saturday

[1] *tabulentur*: 'tabled,' or written on a 'wax-brede.'

mur, laudamus, &c., quod si tempore huius tabulacionis,
* Lf. 13a. scripture aut lecture *eiusdem in capitulo · Decanus pro tempore existens aliquod tale duplex festum pro celebrando ex deuocione licet non tabulatus assumere sibi velit, libere permittatur cum ministris tamen ad officiandum sibi circa altare alias tabulatis contentatus: aliter vero canonicos ad hoc tabulatos nullatenus inquietet, impediat, vel perturbet.

31 = *C.* 27. Nota hic specialem mencionem fieri de Subdecano ante alium presidentem .s. in admissione.

ITEM CUM DE ANTIQUA et prescripta consuetudine ecclesie nostre de qua luculenter informamur, Vicarij per prebendarios eiusdem Ecclesie nostre ad vicarias stallorum suorum in choro Decano et Capitulo presententur, et per Decanum in capitulo aut, ipso Decano absente, per Subdecanum, aut alium presidentem, et capitulum in vicarios huiusmodi admittantur: Cumque cuius seu quorum admissio fuerit seu institucio, illius vel illorum de iure fore dinoscitur destitucio, Arbitramur, &c., quod non [sit] licitum de cetero cuiuis Decano ecclesie nostre predicte vicarios aliquos aut ceteros dicte ecclesie ministros sic vt prefertur per presidentem et capitulum admissos, per se solum, absque communione Capituli, aut ab ecclesie choro, vel aliquo alio iure eidem admisso competente expellere aut ab habitu chori ingressuve ecclesie, aut alicuius emolumenti percepcione preterquam contumacem confessum, aut conuictum causa cognita suspendere vel priuare.

32 = *C.* 32. De annullacione arbitrij per d. [W. Gray].

ITEM CUM BONE MEMORIE Dominus Wyllielmus Gray (A.D. 1434.)
noster predecessor super similibus questionibus et dissensionum materijs nonnullas fecerit declaraciones et ordinaciones inter partes in nos compromittentes, de cuius potestate aliter quam ordinaria, aut partium submissione in ea parte in ipsum facta, nobis non est sufficiens facta

we decide and decree that if at the time of the making of this list or of the writing it down or reading it out at the Chapter, the Dean for the time being wish to take upon himself the celebrating at such double feast out of devotion, even though his name does not so figure in the list, he shall be freely permitted to do so; he being willing nevertheless to be assisted at the altar by those ministers who otherwise were tabled to officiate; but that otherwise he under no circumstances disturb, hinder or upset the Canons to whom these duties have been assigned.

which he is not tabled to celebrate he may do so.

Also, since by an ancient and prescribed custom of our Church, of which we have clear information, the Vicars are presented to the Dean and Chapter by the Prebendaries of the same our Church to the vicarships of their stalls in choir and are admitted as such Vicars by the Dean in Chapter, or if the Dean be away by the Subdean or other President and the Chapter, and since it is recognised in law that the power of deprivation shall rest with the same person or persons to whom the right of admission and institution shall have belonged; we decide etc. that it shall not be lawful henceforward for any Dean of our aforesaid Church to expel competently, by his own sole authority and without communicating with the Chapter, any vicars or other ministers of the said Church who have been so admitted, as has been described above, by the President and Chapter, from fellowship with the Chapter or from the choir of the Church, or from any other right duly conferred on one of the same, or to suspend or deprive him from wearing the choir habit or from entry into the Church or from receiving any emolument, unless after the case has been investigated he be proved contumacious or has confessed, or has been convicted.

C. 27.
31. Vicars duly admitted by President and Chapter not to be deprived by the Dean alone.

Also since the Lord William Grey of blessed memory, our predecessor, on similar grounds and causes of disagreement made several pronouncements and ordinances between the parties assenting to our arbitration; and since we are not sufficiently convinced of his power otherwise than as Ordinary or of the submission made to him by the

C. 32.
32. Certain awards of Bp Will. Grey concerning which there are considerable doubts declared null and void.

fides: Cumque ipsum predecessorem nostrum partibus non vocatis, sed absentibus, ac loco alio quam in dictis ordinacionibus narratiue, submissionem huiusmodi asseritur fore factam, ipsas ordinaciones, siue declaraciones, tulisse reperimus, declaraciones ipsas siue ordinaciones ac omnia in ipsis contenta, nullas et invalidas, nullaque et invalida, ac viribus non subsistere nec subsistere debere, arbitramur, pronunciamus et declaramus.

33 = *C.* 38. De custodia sigilli. [Liber Niger, p. 285.]

ITEM QUIA de more et obseruancia antiquitus in ecclesia nostra vsitatis, ac ex verbis libri consuetudinarij eiusdem ecclesie. sigillum commune remanere debet in Custodia cancellarij, prepositi et vnius canonici residenciarij · Arbitramur, laudamus, &c., quod non liceat neque licebit Decano pro tempore existenti clauem principalem. aliamue ciste in qua reponitur commune Sigillum, sibi vendicare aut exigere: sed sigillum ipsum more antiquo, per cancellarium et alios supradictos debere in posterum conseruari: *et nullatenus per Decanum, nisi loco tercie persone, videlicet Canonici ad hoc per Capitulum ipse Decanus consenciens eligatur quodque non liceat Decano supradicto literas aliquas clausas Decano et capitulo ad exterius indorsatas seu suprascriptas, et eidem Decano porrectas, antequam in Capitulo conueniat cum confratribus capitulariter ad hoc seu ex alia causa conuocandis, aperire · cum litere ipse non sunt sue.

* Lf. 13b.

34 = *C.* 39, 42. ? Formam litterarum subdecani et capituli ipso decano non subesse. Nota hic de Subdecano aut presidente.

ITEM CUM LICEAT Capitulo ecclesie nostre pro iuribus ipsius ecclesie defensandis, et debitis commune vtputa a bonis Decani discretis et separatis exigendis et leuandis, Decano absente non vocato, sub ipsius nomine decanali. nomine proprio aut cognomine minime expresso aut presente et contradicente absque tamen causa racionabili consimiliter sub ipsius nomine aut subdecani, alterius ve presidentis, et capituli nomine, de consuetudine ecclesie

parties in this behalf; and since we find that our predecessor published these ordinances or pronouncements without the parties being called, and in their absence, in a place other than that in which it is stated expressly in the said ordinances that such submission would be made; we decide, make pronouncement and proclaim that these pronouncements and ordinances and all that is contained in them are null and void and neither have nor ought to have any force.

C. 38. 33. The Dean not to have possession of the common seal, nor to open letters addressed to Dean and Chapter except in Chapter.

Also since by the custom and use followed in our Church from ancient times, and from the words of the Consuetudinary of the same Church, the common seal ought to remain in the custody of the Chancellor, Provost and one residentiary Canon; we decide, decree etc. that it be not lawful nor shall be lawful for the Dean for the time being to lay claim to or obtain possession of the chief or other key of the chest in which the common seal is kept; and that the seal itself according to ancient custom be kept for the future by the Chancellor and other persons above referred to; and under no circumstances by the Dean, unless the Dean himself with his own consent be elected by the Chapter to the place of the third person, namely of the Canon chosen for this office by the Chapter. And that it be not lawful for the Dean to open any letters which are sealed and endorsed or addressed on the outside to the Dean and Chapter, and handed to the Dean, before he meet with his brethren in Chapter, summoned Chapter-wise, for this or any other purpose, since the letters themselves are not his own.

C. 39, 42. 34. The Dean not to hinder counsel acting for the Chapter in any civil or spiritual court, under pain of greater excommunication.

Also, since it is lawful for the Chapter of our Church for the defence of the rights of the Church itself or for the recovery and exaction of debts to the common body (as for example those distinct and separate from the property of the Dean), though the Dean be away and not summoned, in the name of the Dean (his Christian and surname not being mentioned), or if he be present and object, so it be without any reasonable cause, likewise in his name, or in the name of the Subdean or other President, and the Chapter, according to the custom of our Church, to

Jurisperiti regni... super procuratorijs ...decanus non asserat prouisionem et can[onicam] futurorum presul[um] censuram.

nostre attornatos et procuratores constituere, vt supra decreuimus et declarauimus (licet aliqui in iure Regio sive Regni periti contrarium senciant pro eorum velle:) Arbitramur, laudamus, &c., quod Decanus quiscunque pro tempore existens attornatos seu procuratores huiusmodi per se solum, absque Capituli communione et consensu in curia aliqua spirituali vel temporali reuocare aut disallocare seu disaduocare non presumat cum hoc non sibi ad commodum vel lucrum aliquod sed ad ecclesie nostre dispendium cedere poterit manifestum: absurdum reputantes et inconueniens, si in tam celebri Collegio et Capitulo persona vnica et singularis, suo proprio sensu innitendo, vtilitatem et prouentum dicte ecclesie nostre contra omnes impedire poterit sine causa. Quod si quis Decanus ecclesie nostre predicte hoc, quod in presenti articulo arbitramur, laudamus, &c., contraire presumpserit; sentenciam excommunicacionis maioris quam tam ex potestate nobis tradita, quam eciam ex auctoritate pontificali et ordinaria, post publicacionem huiusmodi laudi, quam loco trine monicionis canonice succedere volumus et laudamus, exnunc prout extunc et extunc prout exnunc in personam suam in hijs scriptis ferimus vltimam penam aut penas subsequentem seu subsequentes ipsum incurrere volumus ipso facto cuiuscunque Decani in hoc delinquentis absolucionem nobis et successoribus nostris Episcopis Lincolñ solummodo reseruantes.

35. (Cf. p. 70.) De redditibus deputatis ad fabricam. * Lf. 14a.

ITEM QUIA redditus et prouentus ad fabricam dicte Ecclesie nostre deputatos per *minus prouidam gubernacionem eorundem tam magistrorum quam eciam clericorum dicte fabrice, post eorum recepcionem, in mutuis que recuperari non possunt, et donacionibus in dicte ecclesie nostre non modicam lesionem, ac Canonicorum eiusdem presencium et futurorum ineuitabile dispendium comperimus consumptos et mirabiliter dissipatos · Arbitramur, laudamus, &c., quod canonici dicte ecclesie nostre, Magistri videlicet dicte ecclesie fabrice electi et eligendi, dictos redditus et prouentus ad ipsam fabricam pro-

appoint attorneys and proctors, as we have above decreed and declared (though some skilled in the king's law or law of the realm think otherwise as they wish); we decide, decree etc. that no Dean for the time being take upon himself by his own authority without consulting or gaining the consent of the Chapter to revoke or disallow or unbrief such attorneys or proctors in any spiritual or temporal court; since it is not of any benefit or advantage to himself but can result in manifest damage to our Church; since we regard it as ridiculous and incongruous that in so numerous a College and Chapter one individual person by himself, relying on his own initiative, should be able without cause to obstruct the convenience and advantage of our said Church in spite of all the other members. And if any Dean of our said Church shall dare to contravene this which we decide and decree in this present section, we will that he incur *ipso facto* the sentence of greater excommunication (which both by the power handed down to us and by our authority as Bishop and Ordinary after the publication of this award which we will and decree to take the place of the threefold canonical monition we launch from now as from then and from then as from now against his person in these writings), and we will that he incur *ipso facto* the extreme penalty or penalties that follow, and we reserve the absolution of any Dean guilty in this matter to ourselves and our successors the Bishops of Lincoln alone.

35. Moneys belonging to the fabric fund of the Church to be strictly expended on the fabric, and devoted to no other use whatsoever.

Also since we find that the revenues and income set apart for the fabric of our said Church are through lack of careful management on the part both of the masters and clerks of the said fabric used up and marvellously wasted after they are received, in loans which cannot be recovered and donations, to the no little hurt of our said Church and to the inevitable expense of the present and future Canons of the same; we decide and decree etc. that the Canons of our said Church, that is the Masters elected or who shall be elected over the fabric of the said Church, receive into their own hands the revenues and incomings

uenientes et prouenturos, siue in domorum redditibus, siue ex fidelium aliquorum pia deuocione in legatis, aut oblatis, aut alijs emolumentis quibuscunque consistant, ad manus suas proprias recipiant, aut in cista ad hoc disposita reponant pecunias illas in vsum alium aliter quam solum in dicte ecclesie fabricam, et onerum eidem fabrice incumbencium supportacionem, cuiuscunque persone cuiuscunque status fuerit aut condicionis mutuando donando aut aliquo alio modo alienando nullatenus ex quacunque causa exponere aut erogare presumant. Quodque cum ad reparacionem, refeccionem, aut edificacionem ecclesie nostre, aut domorum, expensas aliquas facere oportuerit illas pecunias ad hoc necessarias, clerico dicte fabrice per indenturas exinde inter ipsos et dictum clericum conficiendas tradant et liberent reparaciones huiusmodi et expensas superuisuri quociens et quando commode ad hoc possint intendere. quod si hoc presens laudum nostrum in hac parte non seruauerint, aut non seruauerit aliquis eorundem, contrafacientem ex certa sciencia sentenciam excommunicacionis maioris, preter penas in hac parte ferendas, incurrere volumus ipso facto · quorum et eorum cuiuslibet, absolucionem nobis et successoribus nostris Episcopis Lincolñ specialiter reseruamus.

36 = *C.* 31. De procuracionibus racione visitacionis.

ITEM LAUDAMUS, ordinamus, arbitramur, &c., quod Decanus ecclesie nostre Lincolñ modernus, et singuli eius successores prebendas ecclesie nostre Lincolñ, in quibus de consuetudine aut aliter ius habent visitandi, personaliter visitantes, in exigendis procuracionibus ad huiusmodi[1] vsitatis moderacionem sequantur extrauagantis decretalis que incipit "VAS ELECCIONIS," &c., nisi aliud habeant ex priuilegio speciali.

[Benedict. Papa XII. in *Extrav. Communi*, tit. x. cap. 1. *De censibus, exactionibus et procurationibus*.]

[1] [*Inserendum uidetur* 'visitaciones'.]

accruing or which shall accrue for the fabric itself, whether it be from rents of houses or from the pious devotion of any of the faithful, from legacies, offerings or of whatsoever emoluments they may consist; that they place them in the chest set apart for this purpose; and that under no circumstances shall they dare to dispose of or spend these moneys on any other object than on the fabric of the said Church only and in the bearing of those charges which are incurred in the said fabric, by making a loan to any person whatsoever, whatever his rank and position, by donation or by any other method of alienation. And that when it is necessary to make any expenditure on the repairs, restoration, or building of our Church or houses, they shall hand over and deliver those moneys necessary for this purpose to the clerk of the said fabric by indentures then to be made between them and the said clerk; and that they shall inspect such repairs and expenditure as often as and whensoever they can conveniently look into them. And if they shall not obey this present award of ours in this particular, or if any of them shall not obey it, we will that anyone deliberately acting contrary to it incur *ipso facto* the sentence of greater excommunication, in addition to the penalties to which they are liable in such case; and we specially reserve the absolution of them or any of them to ourself and our successors the Bishops of Lincoln.

36. *C.* 31. The Deans in their visitation of prebends not to exact fees beyond what is their due.

Also we decree, ordain and decide etc. that the present Dean of our Church of Lincoln and each of his successors when they visit in person the prebends of our Church of Lincoln over which, by custom or otherwise, they have the right of visitation, in exacting the usual fees shall follow the guidance of the Extravagant Decretal "*Vas electionis*," etc.[1], unless they are specially privileged otherwise[2].

[1] This decree (*Vas electionis*) was cited subsequently in part i. of the *Novum Registrum* prepared by Bp Alnwick (*Statutes* ed. Bradshaw and Wordsworth, iii. pp. 288–9).

[2] An indult of this kind was granted to Dr Macworth by pope John XXIII. in 1413. *Cal. Papal Letters*, vi. 379.

37. De emolumentis inter decanum &c. per capita diuidendis.
* Lf. 14b.
(*Vide supra*, pp. 17, 72.) See *Lincoln Cathedral Statutes*, (1897) iii. 182, 194. *Vide supra*, p. 8.

ITEM CUM IN LAUDO quondam per bone memorie Dominum Ricardum nuper Lincolñ Episcopum predecessorem nostrum lato inter cetera sic contineatur · "Item quod commoda et prouentus insinuacionum testamentorum infra clausum *Lincolñ et vacacionem prebendarum ad Decanum et capitulum Lincolñ communiter pertineant"; quod quidem laudum a nonnullis reputatur ambiguum et obscurum, asserentibus Decanum facere vnam partem, et Capitulum aliam · sicque emolumenta huiusmodi diuidi debere in duas partes, quarum vnam Decanum, et aliam Capitulum recipere debere affirmant: Nos vero considerantes in ipso laudo contineri aliquorum emolumentorum terciam partem, et aliorum medietatem, Decanum recipere debere per expressum, coniecturamus et conicimus quod si idem predecessor noster medietatem obuencionum veniencium ex insinuacionibus testamentorum, et vacationibus prebendarum, predictum Decanum habere voluisset: modo consimili sicut in ceteris hoc palam expressisset. Quodque ante dictum laudum huiusmodi emolumenta inter Decanum prebendatum residenciarium, et canonicos Capitulum facientes, equaliter diuidebantur, prout ex dictis testium in hac parte productorum liquido informamur; Ac quod in alijs capitularibus tractatibus in quibus exigitur Decanus et Capitulum, Decanus vocum medietatem non optinet, sed solum vnam: Arbitramur, laudamus, &c., predicta emolumenta inter Decanum et Capitulum secundum capita, et nullatenus per partes quotas fore aliqualiter diuidenda.

38 = *C.* 20. De admissione pauperum clericorum ['per decanum' *add. P.*]. Nota hic non fieri mencio-

ITEM CUM DECANUS Ecclesie nostre Lincolñ modernus pauperes clericos ad custodias altarium in ecclesia nostra predicta legere et psallere nescientes, et sic ipsi ecclesie non accommodos. sed magis invtiles, aliquociens inordinato fauore, et aliquando ad quorundam ipsius familiarium munera propter hoc vt dicitur recipiencium instancias recipiat, vt informamur; qui nullo prestito iuramento

37. The income from Probate of wills not to be divided into two parts of which the Dean to take one and the Chapter the other; but to be equally divided *per capita* among the Deans and Canons.

Also since in an award put forth in the past by the Lord Richard late Bishop of Lincoln, our predecessor, among other things this clause occurs: "Also that the profits and revenues from the registration of wills within the close of Lincoln and from the vacancy of prebends belong to the Dean and Chapter of Lincoln in common"; (which award indeed is regarded by some as being indefinite and ambiguous;) and since they assert that the Dean represents one half and the Chapter the other; and that therefore gains arising from such sources ought to be divided into two halves, of which they maintain that the Dean should take one and the Chapter the other; now since we believe that in that award it is clearly laid down that the Dean should receive the third part of some emoluments and the half of others, we are inclined to think that if the same our predecessor had meant the said Dean to have half the proceeds arising from the registration of wills and the vacancy of prebends, he would have expressed himself clearly on this point as on other matters; and since before the time of the said award emoluments arising from these sources were equally divided between the Dean, as holding a residentiary Prebend, and the Canons making up the Chapter (as we are clearly informed by the evidence of witnesses brought forward to prove this point); and since in the deciding of other capitular businesses for which the Dean and Chapter are required, the Dean does not hold half the voting power, but one vote only; we decide and decree that the said emoluments shall be equally divided *per capita* and under no circumstances by so many parts [i.e. in halves (or thirds)].

38. *C.* 20. Clerks not to be appointed to the custodianship of altars by favouritism. All such to take the

Also since the present Dean of our Church of Lincoln accepts for the keeperships of the Altars in our aforesaid Church, as we are told, Poor Clerks, who are unable to read and sing the psalms and so are not suitable for the Church but rather are useless, sometimes by unrestrained favouritism, and sometimes at the insistent pressure of certain of his retainers, who receive bribes (as is reported) for this favour; and that they betake them to

nem de sub-decano, absente decano, sed de capitulo ['viz. quantum ad recepcionem iuramenti' *add. P.*].

ministerijs et officijs huiusmodi clericis pertinentibus se immiscent Arbitramur, laudamus, &c., quod Decanus predictus, et eius successores quicunque, de dictis officijs, ministerijs nullos alios preterquam in lectura et cantu competenter instructos, omnibus fauore et corrupcione postpositis, prouideat et prouideant temporibus vacacionum successiuis: Ipsique clerici sic admissi vel recepti per Decanum, antequam sua officia intrent, vel de eisdem intromittant, coram Decano presente et Capitulo vel ipso decano absente coram capitulo de bene et fideliter faciendo totum, et ea que ad eorum spectant officia supradicta, ad sancta Dei euangelia iurent; aliaque prestent† iuramenta, si que per huiusmodi clericos prestari solita fuerint, et consueta.

† 'pre-[se]ntent' MS.

39. De Juramento obseruacionis huius Laudi. * Lf. 15a.

ITEM ARBI*TRAMUR, &c., quod quiscunque ad quamcunque dignitatem personatum officium vel canonicatum et prebendam, in dicta ecclesia nostra imposterum admittendus; in sui admissione ad huiusmodi dignitatem, personatum, officium, vel Canonicatum et prebendam, preter solitum iuramentum in huiusmodi admissionibus de consuetudine et statuto dicte ecclesie nostre prestari consuetum hoc nostrum laudum, et omnia in eo contenta, quantum in ipso erit, inuiolabiliter obseruabit · nec aliquibus personis volentibus vel nitentibus laudum illud violare vel infringere, seu eidem contraire, dabit assistenciam, auxilium vel fauorem iurare teneatur, et iuret, ac iuramentum prestet corporale, Quodque Decanus et Capitulum, ac singuli canonici dicte ecclesie nostre residenciarij, mox et incontinenter post prolacionem huiusmodi laudi nostri, ipsum nostrum laudum, et omnia in eo contenta, absque aliquo interuallo, et antequam ad aliqua alia extranea se diuertant, emologabunt et emologabit quilibet eorundem: et quod ipsi Decanus et residenciarij inpresenciarum coram nobis, ac singuli alij dignitates, personatus, officia, canonicatus, et prebendas in eadem ecclesia nostra

the duties and offices belonging to such clerks without any oath being required of them; we decide and decree etc. that the aforesaid Dean and all his successors whatsoever, at all times when such vacancies shall occur in future, shall find to perform the said duties [or] offices none other than those who have been sufficiently instructed in reading and singing, all favouritism and corrupt practice being laid aside. And that the clerks themselves so received and admitted by the Dean, before they enter upon their offices or take up the duties of the same, shall swear in the presence of the Dean if present and Chapter, or if the Dean himself be away in the presence of the Chapter, on the holy gospels of God, that they will well and faithfully perform the whole of their duty and those matters which belong to their aforesaid offices; and that they take all other oaths which may be customary, and are wont to be taken by such clerks.

accustomed oaths before they enter upon their duties.

Also we decide etc. that whosoever shall for the future be admitted to any dignity, place, office or canonry and prebend in our said Church on his admission to such dignity, place, office or canonry and prebend, shall in addition to the usual oath accustomed to be taken on such admission by custom and statute of our said Church, be bound to swear, and shall swear, and take his oath in person to keep inviolate this our award and all things contained in it, so far as in him lies; nor shall he give help, assistance or support to any persons wishing or purposing to violate or disobey this award or act against it. And that the Dean and Chapter and each of the residentiary Canons of our said Church shall at once and immediately on the promulgation of this our award, all and each of them swear that they will adhere to this our award and to all things contained in it, without letting any time elapse and before they turn their attention to any other different business; and that the Dean and Residentiaries now themselves before us, and all others not residentiary already possessing dignities, places, offices, canonries and prebends in our same Church who are about

39. All future members of the Body on their admission to swear to observe this award, and the present D. and C. to swear obedience to it immediately on its promulgation.

pro nunc optinentes non residenciarij, residenciam in eadem imposterum facturi maiorem; in sue inicio residencie idem per omnia iuramentum in suis proprijs personis coram toto Capitulo prestent et prestare teneantur, et prestet et prestare teneatur quilibet eorundem.

40. ITEM LAUDAMUS, arbitramur, &c., quod quociens et quando ipse Decanus vel capitulum huiusmodi, aut aliqua singularis persona eiusdem Capituli, predicto nostro laudo, aut alicui capitulo eiusdem contrauenerit, aut contrauenire, seu illud in aliqua sui parte infringere vel eneruare volentibus et nitentibus assistenciam auxilium vel fauorem prebuerit; et ipsum laudum, et quodlibet eius capitulum, *integre et sine diminucione,* sicut illud tulimus, non obseruauerint: tociens viginti libras legalis moneti Anglie fabrice dicte ecclesie Lincolñ nomine pene soluere teneatur, et realiter soluat quilibet eorundem, arbitrio nostro nichilominus firmo manente, et pro maiori securitate solucionis premisse pene, et ne solucio huiusmodi quociens incurratur vllatenus valeat impediri seu differri, Ipsi Decanus et capitulum, communiter vel diuisim, ad eleccionem nostram, securitatem illam de qua vna cum aduisamento iuris regni peritorum et alias prouiderimus; et eisdem Decano et capitulo coniunctim, vel eorum vtrique diuisim, quocunque tempore *infra biennium exnunc proxime futurum, notificauerimus et declara[ueri]mus, sigillabunt, et eidem consencient; literasque in ea parte necessarias et requisitas nobis sub testimonio authentico liberabunt.

Nota. quilibet canonicus qui violauerit debet soluere ecclesie xx[ti] libras.

* Lf. 15b.

OMNIA autem et singula supradicta per nos arbitrata, laudata, diffinita et arbitraliter sentenciata, et pronunciata, dicimus arbitramur et precipimus sub penis superius expressatis in singulis capitulis laudi, si contrafactum fuerit committendum vt predicitur. Et insuper reseruamus nobis nostra auctoritate ordinaria plenariam potestatem super omnibus et singulis per nos arbitratis, laudatis, diffinitis et pronunciatis in presenti arbitrio atque laudo interpretandi atque semel et pluries, et quociens nobis placuerit, vt videbitur expedire.

to keep their greater residence in the same hereafter, shall take and be bound to take at the beginning of their residence the same identical oath in their own persons in the presence of the whole Chapter, and that each of them shall take it and be bound to take it.

Also we decree, decide etc. that as often as and when 40.
the Dean himself or this Chapter, or any individual member of the same Chapter, shall act contrary to this our award or any section of the same, or shall afford any help, assistance or support to those wishing and intending to act against it or disobey it or take away the force of any part of it; and shall not observe the award itself and every section of it wholly and without detraction, as we have put it forth; so often shall he be bound to pay by way of penalty, and either of them, whoever it be, shall actually pay, £20 of lawful money of England to the fabric of the said Church, our decision standing fast all the same. And for the greater security for the payment of the aforesaid penalty, and to prevent the possibility of any delay or obstacle in its payment whenever it be incurred, the Dean and Chapter shall together or separately, as we shall appoint, put their seal to and consent to such security as we shall require on the advice of those skilled in the laws of this realm and otherwise, and as we shall notify and declare to the said Dean and Chapter conjointly, or to each of them separately, at any time within the two years then next ensuing; and they shall execute the documents in such case necessary and required by us legally witnessed.

Now all and singular points aforesaid which have been decided, decreed, determined, adjudged and have pronouncement made thereon, we declare, decide and enjoin, under the penalties above prescribed in each section of the award in the event of any contravention of it. And, moreover, we reserve to ourself by our authority as Ordinary full power, in all and each of the matters ordered, decreed, defined and pronounced upon in this present decision and award, of interpretation and explanation once or more than once and as often as we shall please, as it may seem expedient.

ET PROTESTAMUR palam publice et expresse, quod non intendimus tacite vel expresse per premissa, vel eorum aliquod, vel eorum alicuius pretextu vel accione, iuri, aut iurisdiccioni nostre Episcopali in premissis, vel eorum aliquo quouismodo derogare, Sed quod huiusmodi ius et iurisdiccio episcopalia, eorumque libertates et consuetudines nobis et successoribus nostris premissis vel eorum aliquo non obstante illibata permaneant et illesa.

CUMQUE VOS Capitulum predictum, singularesque persone eiusdem Capituli, laudum, arbitrium, decretum, pronunciacionem, ordinacionem, declaracionem, et diffinicionem nostra predicta per nos sic facta, acceptaueritis, approbaueritis ratificaueritis, et in scriptis tam singulariter quam in communi emologacionis, iuraueritisque et post eciam singulariter, et in communi, ad sancta Dei euangelia per vos corporaliter tacto libro, quod ipsa laudum et arbitrium nostra, ac omnia in eo contenta, quantum in vobis est et erit, inuiolabiliter obseruabitis; nec aliquibus personis volentibus vel nitentibus laudum illud violare vel infringere, seu eidem contraire, dabitis assistenciam auxilium vel fauorem, Vobis igitur et vestrum cuilibet, in virtute iuramenti vestri huiusmodi per vos prestiti et sub penis in eodem laudo latis, firmiter iniungimus et mandamus, quatinus dictum laudum nostrum, ac singula capitula eiusdem, omniaque et singula in eodem laudo contenta, in forma iuramenti vestri predicti firmiter de cetero obseruetis nec in aliquo contraueniatis eidem.

In quorum omnium et singulorum testimonium presentes literas nostras, siue presens publicum instrumentum fideliter exinde confectum et scriptum per Magistrum Thomam Colstone clericum Lincolñ dioceseos, auctoritate
* Lf. 16ª. apostolica notarium publicum, *nostrumque in hac parte actorum scribam, publicari, et in hanc publicam formam redigi, eiusque signo et subscripcione signari, ac nostri sigilli appensione, iussimus roborari.

And we declare publicly, openly and definitely that we do not purpose by what we have not said or by what we have said in the foregoing or in any detail of the foregoing or under colour or by implication of anything we have said, to diminish our episcopal rights and jurisdiction in the matters above dealt with or in any single point of them, but that these episcopal rights and jurisdiction and the liberties and customs thereto belonging remain untouched and unimpaired to ourselves and our successors, notwithstanding what has gone before or any thing in what has gone before.

And inasmuch as you the aforesaid Chapter, and each individual member of the same Chapter, have accepted, approved and ratified our aforesaid award, order, decision, pronouncement, ordinance, proclamation and determining so made by us, both by written bonds of acceptation individually and in common, and also have moreover sworn individually and in common on the holy gospels of God laying your hands upon the Book, that you will keep inviolably our award and decision and all things contained in it so far as in you lies and shall lie; and that you will not give help, succour or support to any individuals who wish or attempt to violate or disobey that award, or to go against it; we therefore strictly enjoin and command you in virtue of this your oath by you sworn, and under the penalties in the same award prescribed, that for the future you strictly keep according to the terms of your aforesaid oath our said award, and each section of the same, and all and singular the things contained in the same award, and that in no point shall you act contrary to it.

And in witness of all and singular these things, we have ordered these present letters, or this present public document, since faithfully drawn up and written out by Mr Thomas Colston, clerk of the Diocese of Lincoln, public notary by apostolic authority, and our secretary and recorder of transactions in this behalf, to be published and reduced into this public form, and to be signed with his signature and subscription and to be confirmed by the setting thereunto of our seal.

(Dated, *Tuesday*, June 23, 1439.) Data et Acta sunt hec omnia et singula prout suprascribuntur et recitantur sub Anno Domini mccccxxxjx. Indiccione secunda pontificatus sanctissimi in Christo patris et domini nostri domini Eugenij diuina prouidencia huius nominis pape quarti anno ·ix°·, mensis Junij die vicesima tercia. Presentibus tunc ibidem discretis viris Magistris

Roberto Thornton Archidiacono Bedeford in dicta ecclesia Lincolñ,

Johanne Depyng canonico dicte Ecclesie nostre Lincolñ in legibus licenciato,

Thoma Ludham et

Alano Humberston eciam canonicis eiusdem ecclesie nostre Lincolñ, et

Johanne Drewell decretorum doctore,

(Sealed, Nettleham, *Monday*, 29 June, 1439.) Testibus vocatis et rogatis specialiter ad premissa, et quo ad sigilli nostri appensionem in Manerio nostro de Nettelham ·xxjx°· die mensis Junij, anno Domini supradicto, Nostrarum consecracionis anno ·xiij· et translacionis tercio./

Ave Maria[1].

ET ego Thomas Colston Clericus Lincolñ dioceseos, publicus auctoritate apostolica Notarius, dictique reuerendi in Christo patris et domini domini Wyllelmi Dei gracia Lincolñ Episcopi, Arbitri, arbitratoris, et diffinitoris predicti in premissis, actorum scriba, premissorum laudi et arbitrij per dictum reuerendum patrem, vt premissum est prolacioni eorundemque laudi et arbitrij approbacioni, ratificacioni, confirmacioni, et emologacioni per dictos canonicos residenciarios capitulum dicte ecclesie Lincolñ vt apparuit facientes factis iuramentorum eorundem canonicorum residenciariorum tam singulariter quam in communi prestacioni, ceterisque premissis omnibus et singulis, dum sic ut premittitur sub anno Domini, Indic-

[1] The motto "*Ave Maria*" is introduced in the horizontal crossing of the capital letter E in this Subscription by the Notary.

All and every of these were given and done as they are above written down and recited, in the year of the Lord 1439, in the second indiction in the ninth year of the Pontificate of our most holy Father in Christ and Lord, the Lord Eugenius, by Divine providence fourth Pope of this name, on the 23rd day of the month of June; there being then and there present the worthy Mr Robert Thornton, Archdeacon of Bedford in the same Church of Lincoln, Mr John Depyng[1], Canon of our said Church of Lincoln, Licentiate in Laws, Mr Thomas Ludham, and Mr Alan Humberstone also Canons of the same our Church of Lincoln, and Mr John Drewell, Doctor of Decrees, as witnesses of the foregoing, specially summoned and called, and of the setting thereunto of our seal at our Manor of Nettleham on the 29th day of the month of June, in the year of our Lord aforesaid, in the thirteenth year of our Consecration and the third of our Translation.

Ave Maria.

And I Thomas Colston Clerk of the Diocese of Lincoln, notary public by apostolic authority and recorder of the transactions of the said reverend Father and Lord in Christ, the Lord William by the grace of God Bishop of Lincoln, the judge, arbitrator and determinator aforesaid in the foregoing, [was present] at the putting forth of the foregoing award and decision by the said reverend Father as is aforesaid and at the approving, ratifying, confirming and at the acceptance of the same award and decision by the aforesaid Canons residentiary making up as it appeared the Chapter of the said Church of Lincoln; [I was present] at the taking of the oaths by the same Canons residentiary both individually and in common, and at all and singular the doings aforesaid, while as is aforesaid they were in process of being accomplished and brought about in the year of the Lord, the indiction,

[1] J. Depyng appears as papal mandatory (with the prior of Barnwell) to the confirmation by Eugenius IV., 18 Sep. 1433, of (spurious) privileges to the University of Cambridge. *Cal. Papal Letters*, viii. pp. 484, 485.

cione, pontificatu, mense, et die proxime predictis, in domo Capitulari dicte ecclesie Lincolñ per prefatum Reuerendum Patrem, et coram eo agebantur et fiebant; et prout in hijs quinque pecijs pergameni simul consutis et signo meo solito et consueto super consuturas earundem signatis conscribuntur; vna cum prenominatis testibus presens personaliter interfui eaque omnia et singula sic fieri vidi et audiui et per alium me aliunde occupato fideliter scripta de mandato eiusdem Reuerendi patris Arbitri predicti publicaui, et in hanc formam redegi; meque hic subscripsi,

ac signo et nomine meis consuetis et solitis vna cum appensione sigilli dicti Reuerendi patris expost facta de eius mandato signaui, rogatus et requisitus, in fidem et testimonium omnium et singulorum premissorum. Constat michi notario predicto de interlineari harum diccionum "ecclesie," "meum," "huius nominis," "pondus[1]," "pene declarandi," superius in presenti instrumento; et huius

[1] "pondus" occurs on p. 118 l. 11 of this present edition; "vidi" on l. 7 above, "huius nominis" on p. 78, l. 15, and p. 96, ll. 5, 6; and again on p. 144, l. 5. The words "pene declarandi," etc. might, no doubt, be easily found if the exemplar which Thomas Colston had before him should some day come to light.

pontificate, month and day last mentioned, in the Chapter-House of the said Church of Lincoln by the aforesaid Reverend Father and in his presence; and as they are written out in these five sheets of parchment sewn together and signed over the seams with my usual and accustomed notarial mark; I was present in person with the afore-named witnesses and all and singular these things I saw and heard to be so done, and after they were faithfully written down by another (while I was otherwise occupied), I have published them by command of the same Reverend Father the aforesaid maker of the award; and have reduced them into this public form, and here I have subscribed myself[1] and have signed my usual and accustomed notarial mark and name together with the setting thereunto afterwards of the seal of the said Reverend Father at his command, as I was bidden and requested, in proof and witness of all and singular of the foregoing matters.

And I the said notary public am aware of the interlining of these words 'ecclesie,' 'meum,' 'huius nominis,' 'pondus,' 'pene declarandi' above in this document; and

[1] Thomas Colston's name is here written in the base of an interlaced cross, some three inches high, which is evidently his notarial mark (*signum*) and usual mode of signature.

diccionis "Vidi" in presenti mea subscripcione; nec non de rasura harum diccionum "de de bere libras" et de rasura in xxx[a] linea quarte pecie huius instrumenti, inter dicciones "Nostre" et "Vel"; et de rasura in capite ljx[e] linee quinte pecie eiusdem instrumenti factis: que omnia approbo, et omni suspicione sinistra carere volo.

FINIS LAUDI

of this word 'Vidi' in my subscription here; as also the erasure of these words 'de de bere libras,' and the erasure made in the 30th line of the 4th sheet of this document between the words 'Nostre' and 'vel'; and the erasure made at the beginning of the 59th line of the 5th sheet; all of which I approve, and I desire them to be free from all suspicion of any evil intent.

END OF THE AWARD

M. PARKER'S '*CONTENTA IN LAUDO.*'

The following Table of Contents of the xvth century *Laudum* of Bp W. Alnwick, and more particularly of matters noted in the articles of his award itself, was written in the middle of the xvith century and not improbably while Matthew Parker was Dean of Lincoln, 1552—1554. It is prefixed to Colston's certified text of the *Laudum* itself preserved among the Lincoln Chapter muniments (A. 2. 6), and printed in the present volume. This old Table of Contents shows how Alnwick codified the decisions of his Award in the *New Register* which he began to prepare soon afterwards. It may also serve to show what points were considered to be important or interesting in the opinion of one of Macworth's successors a century after he and Bishop Alnwick had passed away.

Contenta in laudo W. Alnwick, episcopi Lincolniensis, A.D. 1439. [PAGE (*in this edition,* A.D. 1913)

[1] Perhaps 'sicut.'

[2] The numerals in Parker's references to the *pages* of *Novum Registrum* are, of course, about double of the leaf-numerals, or earliest foliation, duly indicated in the margin of H. Bradshaw and C. Wordsworth's edition (Camb. 1897) Part II., *Lincoln Cathedral Statutes*, tom. iii. pp. 268, &c. The cross-reference in *Nov. Reg.* for this 1st Article of the *Laudum* will be found in *Linc. Cath. Stat.* iii. p. 337.

[1] Bp Alnwick having treated the 7th and 8th of the Dean's *grauamina* in one article, the 7th, the later articles of his *laudum* have in this table been at some time numbered one in advance.

*** To Matthew Parker may probably be attributed, not only the foregoing summary of *Contenta in Laudo*, but also such of the *marginalia* as we have marked '*P*,' or '*Parker*'

(and perhaps some others). He may likewise have been responsible for *underlining* those passages (on pp. 90, 98, 102, 112, 120 and 140) which are marked by the use of *italic type*, and also for certain special marks, of which some specimens will be found on p. 98 (*margin*) and p. 130. Similar marks appear in the margin of the MS. (A. 2. 6) in reference to a few other passages of the final Award itself, viz. in sections 17, 18 (*bis*), 20 and 21 (*in fine*),—see pp. 114, 116, 118, 120, and 122 of the present edition,—at the points where Bishop Alnwick made reference to the Lincoln Custom-book or Register, or where some noticeable phrase occurs.

CHRONOLOGICAL NOTES

ON LINCOLN CATHEDRAL PRIVILEGES, CUSTOMS, STATUTES, DISPUTES, AND AWARDS, A.D. 1090–1451.

*** The authorities principally referred to in the following list are:

C.P.L. = *Calendar of Papal Letters*, in Papal Registers relating to Great Britain and Ireland, A.D. 1198–1447, vols. i–ix, edited by W. H. Bliss, C. Johnson, and J. A. Twemlow, 1893–1912[1].

L.C.S. = *Lincoln Cathedral Statutes*: the Black Book, and others, in 3 tomes, edited by H. Bradshaw and Chr. Wordsworth, 1892–1897. Cambridge University Press.

1090. Sept. Charter granted to Remigius Bp of Lincoln by K. William Rufus. *L.C.S.* ii. pp. 1–6.

1214. 'Dignitates, libertates et consuetudines' were registered in the Lincoln *Martilogium* (now lost). Copy sent to Moray. *L.C.S.* ii. 137–160.

1236–7. 'Statuta Vicariorum et Capitula de Residentia.' *L.C.S.* ii. 143–146; 150–160.

1239. Sept. 7. Bp Rob. Grosseteste issues mandate summoning Dean Roger de Wesham and Chapter to attend a visitation on Thursday Oct. 20th. He assures the D. and C. that he will visit them, armed not only with ordinary authority but with that of the Pope. Grosseteste's *Epistles*, No. lxxx. pp. 253–260. (See also *Epist.* cxxvi. p. 357.) On Oct. 7 D. and C. hold a Chapter-meeting, and write round to other cathedrals, and on Sunday, October 9, in cathedral '*ad pulpitum*' obtain leave from the people to appeal to Rome against the Bp. Instead of appearing the Four Principal *Personae* start for Rome. Finding no one in his cathedral on visitation-day, and having business with Abp Edmund of Abingdon in London (for Nov. 3), Grosseteste follows them and finds his friend the Dean and the three other *Personae* and some other canons in town. They, having refused two of his propositions—(*a*) to consult Otho the legate, or (*b*) to send

[1] We are especially indebted to Mr Twemlow for most considerately allowing us the opportunity of reading in proof his summary of documents concerning Lincoln for the years 1447—1451.

messengers to the Pope—agree at length to petition Gregory IX to commit the enquiry to (Wa. de Cantilupe) Bp of Worcester, and archdeacons (W. Scott de Stichill and Alan de Beccles) of Worcester and Sudbury (*u.s.* p. 259). Letter from Grosseteste to S. de Arderne his proctor at Rome, whom he has informed, by W. de Hemmyngburg [cf. *L.C.S.* ii. p. clvii], that he had suspended Dean, Precentor and Subdean from entering the church because of their refusal to withdraw their mandate forbidding vicars and chaplains at prebends and churches *de communa* to comply with his visitation. *u.s.* p. 253.

(?) 1240. Rob. de Hertford D. of Sarum and Salisbury Chapter implore Grosseteste to consent to reconciliation with his Chapter of L. Bp replies (*Epist.* xciii. pp. 290, 291) that the peace which he desires is a *true* one.

(?) 1241. Bp Grosseteste has excommunicated Master Nicholas, proctor for the D. and C., and, when they complain, he reminds them how *they* have excommunicated the Dean [whom he appointed over them], and how they have broken the truce between the Bp and C. by employing Odo de Kilkenny [founder of Lincoln Carmelites] in the King's court. *Epist.* xciv. pp. 293, 294.

1243. Oct. 21. Faculty to Master Richard, canon of L., proctor of D. and C., to contract a loan of 100 marks in their name to pay expenses in Rome and for journey back to England. *C.P.L.* i. 202.

1243. Oct. 23. Innocent IV dispenses Dean (Roger de Wesham), Precentor, Chancellor and Treasurer of L., and rehabilitates them as they have acted not in malice but in simplicity in making arrangement with the Bp without consent or authority from Chapter, in dispute about visitation of Chapter. Their dispute on such points had been committed by Pope Gregory IX to (Wa. de Cantilupe) Bp of Worcester, and others. *C.P.L.* i. 202.

1243. Dec. 22. Mandate to priors of Ely and Wartre and archd. of Rochester. The D. and C. of L. have appealed to the Pope from decision of Bp of Worcester, etc. If Bp (of L.) renounces the process since the appeal, the priors are to relax provisionally the sentences against the Chapter, and fix a term of three months for appearance at Rome. If Grosseteste refuses to renounce process, mandatories are to proceed according to the form sent them. *C.P.L.* i. 203, 204.

1245. Grosseteste writes to tell W. de Raleigh, Bp of Winchester, and Walter de Cantilupe, Bp of Worcester, that he has arrived safely at Lyons, and has been well received by Innocent IV and cardinals. *Epist.* cxiii. p. 333.

1245. Aug. 25. Pope Innocent IV notifies (Rob. Grosseteste) Bp of L. of his pronouncement that the Bp be admitted to visit the D. and C., canons, clerks choral, ministers, vicars of the churches of the chaplains, and their parishioners; and to correct abuses. Canons, however, are not bound to take an oath of obedience. *C.P.L.* i. 219. (The so-called 'Award of Pope Innocent IV.' *L.C.S.* i. 117, 119, no. 26; i. 315–318.)

1245. Oct. 14. On or before this date Grosseteste hopes to land in I. of Wight on his return from Lyons. *Epist.* cxiv. p. 325 (Rolls Series). He had been at Lyons on January 7th. Cant. York Soc. *Rot. Rob. Grosseteste*, Itinerary, p. xii.

1246. Jan. 23. Bp Grosseteste intends to visit the Chapter on this day. He writes *Epist.* cxxi. to explain to Dean H. de Lexinton and Chapter why he is visiting Archdeaconry of Stow before he visited them: replying to complaint brought by Rob. de Bedford, precentor, that Bp said in Chapter that he would begin his visitation with themselves. *Epp.* pp. 343, 344.

cir. 1260. 'Consuetudinarium de Divinis officiis' committed to writing in the time of Ric. Gravesend Bp. *L.C.S.* i. 362–396.

1261. The Composition between Boniface Abp of Canterbury and the D. and C. of L. on jurisdiction *sede vacante.* *L.C.S.* i. 311–315.

1264. The Statute '*De Statu Puerorum.*' *L.C.S.* iii. 161, 162.

1272. Sept. 20. W. Lexington dies. His obit, see p. 124.

1284. March 9. The Statute *De Thesauraria.* *L.C.S.* i. 286, 287.

1294–1304. Statutes of St Paul's, London. (Edition, by Dr W. Sparrow-Simpson, privately printed, for the D. and C., 1873.)

1314. July 27. The Award of J. de Dalderby, Bp. *L.C.S.* i. 319–322.

cir. 1330. The *Liber Niger* or Lincoln Black Book of Customs, etc. is written.

Before 1333. 'Consuetudines non antehac redactae in scripturam.' *L.C.S.* iii. 163–474.

cir. 1333, 1334. The Award of Pope John XXII between Antony Beek, Dean—afterwards (1336–1343) Bp of Norwich—and the Chapter of Lincoln.

1335–1341. Dispute between Ant. Beek, Dean, (J. de Nottingham, and W. Bateman, successively Deans) and the Chapter of L. before the papal court at Avignon.

1335. Dec. 4. Mandate from Benedict XII to prior of Wartre, Denys Haverel (Avenel) archd. of E. Riding and Rob. de Valons, canon of York, to have copies made of the Register or Consuetudinary of L. and other

instruments relating to a cause touching visitation of canons, vicars, and beneficiaries now pending before the Pope between Ant. Beek, papal chaplain, Dean, and the Chapter. Copies to be sent under seal to Avignon. *C.P.L.* ii. 520. On Mar. 13, 1336, the mandatories are called upon to summon the Dean and the canons who have kept back the Register and Customary. *C.P.L.* ii. 529.

1346. May 10. Indult from Pope Clement VI to Ric. de Pulham, chaplain of St Peter's altar, to receive fruits of chaplaincy for three years while non-resident from L. on service of (W. Bateman) Bp of Norwich. *C.P.L.* iii. 211.

1346. July 26. Award of J. Stratford, Abp of Canterbury, *de custodia altaris S. Petri in ecclesia cathedrali Lincoln. L.C.S.* i. 353–361.

1390. W. Courtenay, Abp of Canterbury, holds visitation, *sede Lincoln vacante.* Twelve monitions issued thereupon. *L.C.S.* iii. 245–249.

1395. May 19. Indult for 10 years from Boniface IX to J. Schepeye, Dean of Lincoln, D.C.L., to take fruits of Nassyngton prebend and the deanery, etc. provided he reside one month yearly at L. (instead of 36 weeks at no small expense). *C.P.L.* iv. 526.

1398. Sept. 1. Boniface IX confirms the immemorial custom which Pope Innocent III had confirmed to the canons resident as then having obtained for 40 years or more, whereby the [septisms, or] seventh portion of the revenues of prebends of canons who do not reside during a third part of the year were payable to the Chapter. D. and C. to have power to sequestrate revenues of non-resident canons till the septisms be paid. *C.P.L.* v. 169.

1400. Dec. 2. K. Henry IV directs H. Beaufort Bp, to settle disputes between J. Shepeye Dean, and the canons. *L.C.S.* iii. 250–252.

1400. Dec. 6. Statute and Ordinance of Boniface IX (*subsequently cancelled* by mandate of the Pope) that visitation of the Chapter, reformation, correction, presentation, collation, deprivation, admission, institution, and induction, shall belong conjointly to the Dean, Sub-Dean, Chapter (or any other who presides over the Chapter *add. margin*), notwithstanding Dean Schepey's assertion that these belong to him singly and not conjointly. *C.P.L.* v. 460, 461.

1402. Nov. 17. Ordinance of Pope Boniface IX on petition of perpetual vicars in Lincoln Church, that they may at pleasure, and as often as expedient, say the canonical hours and especially mattins with candles provided at their own expense, statutes and customs to the contrary notwithstanding. *C.P.L.* v. 592, 593.

1403. Dec. 11. '*Nova ordinacio de pastu ministrorum.*' *L.C.S.* iii. 178–180.

1404. July 30. The Award of H. Beaufort, Bp, between Dean J. Shepeye and his Chapter. *L.C.S.* iii. 252, 253. K. Henry IV gives certificate thereof to Sub-dean and Chapter, 16 Nov. 1405. Chapter Muniments, roll A. 2. 10 (No. 4, part iii.).

1404. Decisions of the Court of Rome on jurisdiction given to the Dean of Lincoln in respect of his oath of obedience. 2 membranes of a roll in L. Chapter Muniments, box "*Statuta...Macworth,*" A. 2. 10 (3).

1405. March 7. Dean J. de Schepeye has recently petitioned for the confirmation of Pet. Fabri's sentence [1341; *L.C.S.* iii. 242]. Pope Innocent VII orders (T. Arundel) Abp of Canterbury, the Bp of Tuy, and (Roger Walden) Bp of London, to cause it to be observed by the Chapter, who under pretext of letters of Boniface IX despoiled Dean S. of rights adjudged to the Dean by Fabri, who was auditor appointed by Benedict XII on appeal from the Chapter against the sentence of Pet. de Talliata, papal chaplain and auditor, in favour of Ant. Boeck and W. [Bateman] de Norwico, Deans of L. [1340–1341]. *C.P.L.* vi. 30, where Mr J. A. Twemlow refers back to *C.P.L.* ii. 520, 529; v. 460. [1335, 1336: 1400.]

1405. March 7. Innocent VII annuls letters of Boniface IX ('*Quanto propensius*') 6 Dec. 1400, and orders them to be cancelled from papal register and the originals to be sent back from Lincoln and elsewhere, because they omit reference to the sentences of P. de Talliata and P. Fabri, both of which were in favour of the Dean's sole jurisdiction, especially when present and not negligent. Fabri, however, added saving clauses as to any case of the Dean's absence for three successive days, or of his manifest neglect. *C.P.L.* vi. 30, 31.

1405. Oct. 2. Innocent VII grants an indult to J. de Shepeye, Dean of Lincoln, for two years to reside at Nassyngton, spending one month only (instead of the usual 36 weeks) at L. *C.P.L.* vi. p. 8.

1405. Aug. 8. Monition to Dean Shepeye from K. Henry IV concerning the dispute between D. and C. (apud castrum de Pountfreyt, an. reg. 6). On roll in Linc. Chapter Muniments, box "*Stat. B. V. M. Lincoln:—Dean Macworth,*" A. 2. 10 (No. 4, part iv.).

1410. May 27. Pope John XXIII grants dispensation to J. Macworth, archdeacon of Dorset, to hold another archdeaconry or some benefice or dignity 'incompatible' together with one archdeaconry. Macworth is in litigation in the apostolic palace with regard to archdeaconry of Norwich. He has held a five years' dispensation from

the (deposed) Pope Gregory XII (cir. 1406–9). *C.P.L.* vi. 211.

1410. June 6. Pope John XXIII, on petition of H. de Minutolo, Card. Bp of Sabina and canon of Lincoln, etc., deals with neglect of Hospitallers to pay a cess called septisms, due yearly to the D. and C. on account of prebend of Kynges Sutton and chapels of Bulthorle and Hornton annexed. *C.P.L.* vi. 196, 197. [Innocent IV, Dec. 1251, confirmed the custom whereby for 40 years one seventh is paid to residents by those canons who do not keep four months' residence. *C.P.L.* i. 275.]

1411. July 31. Indult of plenary remission granted by John XXIII to J. Macworth, archd. of Dorset. *C.P.L.* vi. 328.

1411. Oct. 19. Indult (in two forms) granted by John XXIII to Philip Repynton, Bp of L., to visit [D. and C. and] their prebends, etc. and receive procurations notwithstanding an indult granted *c.* 1245 by Innocent IV to exempt from procurations. *C.P.L.* vi. 245 and 299. Cf. *L. C. Stat.* iii. 277, *Nov. Reg.* part i. margin; ii. p. clx, *n.*

1412. John Macworth, doctor of canon law, who had been collated to the prebend of Empingham 18 Oct. 1404, was installed to that canonry 26 Apr. 1412, and entered upon the deanery about the same date in succession to J. de Shepeye. *Fasti*, Le Neve-Hardy, ii. 33, 147.

1413. Jan. 5. Mandate from Pope to (W. of Colchester), abbot of Westm., to decide the cause on petition of Mr Ric. Derham, papal notary, complaining that J. M., dean of L., has despoiled him of his prebend of Preston in the church of Salisbury. *C.P.L.* vi. 366.

1413. May 15. Indult from John XXIII to J. Macworth for seven years to visit his archdeaconry (Dorset in dio. Sarum) by deputy and receive on one day in ready money several procurations. '*Sincere deuocionis affectus.*' *C.P.L.* vi. 379. (Cf. 'Divisim ministrarunt,' p. 66 *n.*, above.)

1418. March 23. Mandate issued by Pope Martin V to the prior of Barnwell to absolve Dean Macworth (enjoining a penance) from an oath which he and the Chapter took when he (as preb. of Empingham, archd. of Dorset) and they were assembled for election of a Dean of Lincoln, viz. that the person who should be elected would renounce all bulls, etc. obtained by the late dean (J. Schepeye) against the Chapter; the said oath being prejudicial to the deanery. '*Circa fidelium.*' *C.P.L.* vii. p. 65.

c. 1418 (or ? earlier, 1412–20). Award of Philip Repyngdon, Bishop, on dispute between Dean Macworth and Chapter. *L.C.S.* i. 260, 261. Articles submitted to T. Langley, Bp of Durham, P. Repyngdon, Bp of L., and Mr H. Ware

as arbiter, by the Chapter against Dean Macworth are among L. Chapter Muniments A. 2. 10 (5), box "*Statuta B. V. M. Lincoln: Dean Macworth.*"

1419–20. Among faculties for conferring the *officium tabellionatus* (of notary) in Feb.–Oct. such were issued in favour of T. Atkyn, clerk, not married, Ro. Lockyng, married clerk, and W. Kyrkby, clerk, not married, and not in holy orders. *C.P.L.* vii. p. 147. (Cf. the faculty for clerks—'not married and not in holy orders'—issued to Rob. Fytz Hugh, archd., in Sept. 1423. *u.s.* vii. p. 272.)

1420. Oct. 8. Indult from Pope Martin V to J. Macworth, B. Canon Law (and formerly Chancellor of K. Henry when Prince of Wales); to let and farm the fruits of the deanery and other benefices, or otherwise use them for purposes of repair of buildings of such benefice, during the Pope's pleasure, whilst studying letters at an university, or during five years whilst in service to the King, or residing in the Roman court, or on one of the benefices annexed to deanery. '*Litterarum,*' etc. *C.P.L.* vii. pp. 146, 147. (Mandate concurrent to Bp of Condom, Bp of London, and prior of Barnwell.)

1421. April 15. Award of Bp Ric. Fleming delivered at Lincoln. It was sealed by Bp Fleming in London, May 27, and subsequently confirmed by the King's Letters Patent at Westm., May 30, 1421. This award, on the legitimate interpretation of certain phrases in the Black Book relating to separate or common jurisdiction of the D. and C., was pronounced by Bp in presence of K. Henry V. See *L.C.S.* i. 147, 148.

1423. June 15. Indult *de litteris ante diem* granted by Pope Martin V to J. Macworth, Dean of Lincoln: to have mass before daybreak. *C.P.L.* vii. p. 315.

1423. Nov. 6. Mandate of Pope Martin V to [W. Alnwick] archdeacon of Salisbury: granted by Pope Martin V at petition of J. Macworth, Dean, and Chapter of Lincoln to confirm the *ad valorem* assessment of amount to be paid by canons to the dean for visitation procurations in respect of their prebends, instead of the old custom whereby each canon paid the same amount irrespective of the value of his prebend. '*Humilibus supplicum.*' *C.P.L.* vii. pp. 272, 273.

1423. Nov. 6. Mandate of Pope Martin V to Bp of Durham and Bp of London to confirm arbitration by Bp Ric. [Fleming] in the long-standing controversy between predecessors of Dean Macworth and predecessors of J. Percy, Subdean, and Chapter, as to visitation of Church of Lincoln, its prebends, etc., and use of episcopal jurisdiction *sede vacante.* Litigation has long

gone on, in England first, and afterwards in the apostolic palace, in which latter definitive sentences have been given, the appeal from the last of which was before a papal auditor, who had proceeded short of a conclusion, when the said parties agreed to have recourse to Bishop Richard's arbitration, the terms of which are contained in a public instrument (not here exemplified). '*Hiis que pro statu.*' *C.P.L.* vii. 272.

1434. Sept. 27. Award pronounced in the Chapter-house by W. Grey, Bp (translated, 29 Apr. 1431, from London), on dispute between D. and C. It consists of 41 articles, but was ineffectual, the Bp having neglected to take certain preliminary steps before its delivery. *L.C.S.* i. 149.

1434. Nov. 6. Mandate from Eugenius IV to abbot of Derham, Norfolk, and prior of Ely, to summon Dean Macworth and Rob. Cayngham, a priest whom Macworth employed for excommunicating four canons of Lincoln, though having no jurisdiction over them. They are to absolve the said canons, viz. J. Southam (archd. Oxon., 1404–1438), J. Haget (treasurer 1406–1442), J. Heth (preb. of Castor 1414–1443, previously subdean, archd. of Huntingdon), and Ric. Ingoldesby (preb. of Welton Bekhall, a residentiary), conditionally (*ad cautelam*) and, after hearing both sides, to decide without appeal, to dispense them on account of irregularity and rehabilitate them. *C.P.L.* viii. p. 497.

1435. June 28. T. Atkyn, notary, and seven armed retainers of Dean Macworth assault Chancellor Peter Partrich at evensong in choir, drag him out of his stall, by his almuce, on to a bench and tear his habit. *Record Commission Report* xiv. app. viii. p. 21. *L.C.S.* iii. p. clxxxviii, *n.*

1435. Aug. 23rd and 24th. Five documents relating to the dispensations granted by Eugenius IV to 'Rob. Burtoneñ,' precentor of Lincoln, S.T.M., to hold incompatible benefices, etc., with Stebbenhith rectory (Stepney) in the diocese of London, archd. of Northumberland, and Bliburgh R., in dio. Linc.; an indult for life to visit his archdeaconry by deputy, to let his benefices to farm, if non-resident studying letters in an univ., or being in service of the King, or the Duke of Gloucester, or a prelate. *C.P.L.* viii. p. 285.

1435. Oct. 14. Mandatė issued by the official of Canterbury to cite Dean Macworth. Similar mandate 'ex parte Petri Partrich cancellarii eccl. Linc.' to cite the Dean and his servants on a charge of violence. *Registr. W. Grey, Epi.* f. 181. See above, June 28. The case was brought before the civil court at Westminster in Hilary term, 1436. *L.C.S.* iii. p. clxxxviii, *n.*

1436. W. Alnwick, LL.D. Cam., O.S.B., archd. of Sarum (1420–1426), Bp of Norwich (cons. 18 Aug. 1426), confessor to nuns at Syon and to K. Henry VI, is translated to the see of Lincoln after the death of Bp Grey which took place late in Feb. 1436. Royal assent to Alnwick's election 23 May, notified to Pope Eugenius IV, who sends bull of provision 19 Sept. 1436. *Regist. Chichele*, f. 54 (*Fasti*, Le Neve-Hardy, ii. 18). Temporalities restored, 16 Feb. 1437.

1436. Oct. 21. Faculty from Pope Eugenius IV to W. [Alnewick] Bp of Lincoln: for three years, to visit his diocese by deputy and receive the procurations. *C.P.L.* viii. p. 261.

1437. Oct. 1st to 8th. Bp Alnwick holds his primary visitation in cathedral. *Detecta et comperta* sent in and noted. On Oct. 3rd to 8th Rob. Thornton, as Bp's commissary, examines 83 ministers of cathedral (vicars, sacrist, poor clerks, vergers and bell-ringers, besides choristers, porter, rector and parishioners of St M. Magdalen, and others). *L.C.S.* iii. 364–415.

1438. January 18. Bp Alnwick holds a preliminary investigation (*inquisicio preparatoria*) in the Chapter-house. Petitions of the Dean and Dignitaries are handed in to him. *Detecta et comperta. L.C.S.* iii. 422–425.

1438. June 7. The canons promise under oath to abide by the proposed *Laudum* or Award to be pronounced by Bp Alnwick on or before June 24th. See above, p. 76.

1438. June 16. Dean Mackworth promises to abide by the proposed *Laudum*. See above, p. 94.

(?) 1438. Sept. 19. Pope Eugenius IV (anno 8°) writes to W. Alnwick, bidding him take oath of fealty before receiving possession of administration of the goods of the see of Lincoln. *C.P.L.* viii. p. 612. (Is there not some confusion as to the year—1436 or 1438—either in the Papal Register or in the Chichele Register as cited by Hardy? (*Fasti*, ii. 18 *n.*—Chr. W.)

1438. Sept. 27. Pope Eugenius IV (anno 8°) has received letters of W. (Alnwick) Bp of L. excusing himself (on the ground of penal statute of the realm) from appointing Peter Barbo the Pope's nephew to the prebend of Sutton [*cum* Bucks.], void by consecration of W. Ayscough to the see of Salisbury. Bp of L. ought by reason of his oath to obey the Pope's mandate, and he may do so because the Pope has ordered provision to be made of another canonry [Langford manor], which is vacant by the death of Mr Rob. Sutton at the Roman court, for T. Bekynton, for whom K. Henry VI seemed anxious to obtain that canonry. '*Rescripsisti nobis.*' *C.P.L.* viii. 266. (Bp Alnwick, however collates Nic. Dixon to Sutton stall,

29 July, 1438; also T. Coles to Langford Manor, 17 Nov. 1439. P. Barbo was archd. of Sarum, 1444–1446.) The Pope wrote on the aforesaid matter to K. Henry on Sept. 29, and to the Duke of Gloucester on Oct. 1st, 1438. *C.P.L.* viii. 264, 266. Also, on Sept. 28, he wrote to Abp of Canterbury and Bp of London, to receive usual oath of fealty from W. Alnwick, translated to L. from Norwich, dwelling in those parts, so as to save him a visit to Rome; the oath to be returned to the Pope as usual. '*Cum nos nuper.*' *C.P.L.* viii. p. 582.

1439. June 8. Visitation sermon preached by T. Duffield, B.D., Chancellor of L. Meeting of residents and non-residentiary canons, as summoned by Bp. They accept his *Laudum.* He tells them of his intention that a new Book of Statutes should be made and a Fabric Fund begun. *L.C.S.* iii. 427–430.

1439. June 9. At a meeting in the Chapter-house it is agreed that a new Book of Statutes be compiled. *L.C.S.* iii. 430–436.

1439. June 11. An adjourned *convocatio*, at which the assent of T. Beckington (Bp of Bath and Wells), as archd. of Bucks., is made by proxy. *L.C.S.* iii. 437.

1439. June 23. The LAUDUM or Award of BP ALNWICK is pronounced and attested. It was sealed by the Bishop at Nettleham Manor on June 29th. See above, p. 144[1].

1440. March 10. A discussion held concerning visitation of prebends. *L.C.S.* iii. 479.

1440. June 24. Dean Macworth issues mandate, calling non-residentiaries to conference preparatory to visitation. He applies to D. and C. of Salisbury to send a statement of Sarum privileges. (See Aug. 25.) *L.C.S.* i. 402. (*Liber Niger.*)

1440. July 28th and 29th. Vicars choral and other chaplains present statement of grievances. *L.C.S.* iii. 439–443.

1440. Aug. 25. Dr Nic. Bildeston, Dean, and the C. of Salisbury, at Dean Macworth's request, furnish him and the Chapter of L. with a statement of Sarum Privileges, cir. 1091, 1262, 1319, and 1392[2]. *L.C.S.* i. 404–407. (*Liber Niger.*)

1440. Oct. 3. At a second adjourned meeting, Dean Macworth urges the precedence of Sarum immunities, which Bp Alnwick disputes. *L.C.S.* iii. 445.

1440. Oct. 7. A representation is made against Dean Macworth for making a stable over the Cathedral Library.

[1] Alnwick's *Laudum* was fortified by Act of Parliament, 12 Nov. 1439. See note 2 on p. 29, *supra*.

[2] See also the *Copia transumpti transmissi canonicis Lincoln., super ordinacionibus prebendarum Sar.* in Symon Hutchins' Register pp. 22, 23 at Salisbury (25 Aug. 1440).

1440. Bp Alnwick delivers parts i.–iv. of his 'new book' (*Novum Reg.*) to the Chapter-clerk. *L.C.S.* iii. 448.

1440. Oct. 7 in Chapter-house, and 21 Oct. in Lydyngton prebendal church, Bp Alnwick gathers D. and C. round him to discuss and carry out his project to render Tateshale parish church, which has been neglected or at times served by unfit chaplains, a collegiate hospital church. The Dean introduces the subject of visitation of prebends. *L.C.S.* iii. 447, 448; *C.P.L.* ix. 160–163.

1440. Oct. 8. The Dean withdraws from an adjourned meeting. Canons consent to examine *Novum Registrum* further. *L.C.S.* iii. 449.

1441. Apr. 24. The Dean refuses to remove his new stables or to pay rent for them, or to agree to the *Novum Registrum*, and makes his protest before the Bp's Commissary. The Precentor demurs to a regulation in the new book, about fruits of a prebend after the canon's decease. The Bp points out that his book agrees here with the Black Book which they swear to observe. Precentor Burton says the custom is contrarient. On Peter Irford's suggestion the Bp nominates a committee of five experts: Precentor Burton, Chanc. Partrich, Ric. Ingoldesby, J. Marshall residents, and J. Depyng non-res., and prorogues the meeting (*convocationem*) till 9 April, 1442. *L.C.S.* iii. 450–453.

1441. Oct. 15. Holy Trinity Tateshale is made collegiate. *C.P.L.* ix. 159.

1442. Apr. 9. At a Chapter-meeting (D. and six residentiaries only present who answer subsequently as proxies for the rest) T. Ryngsted, as commissary, reads a letter from the Bp, whose absence he explains. They adjourn till afternoon ('*post nonas*'), when Dean Macworth said, 'My brethren, we have a handsome papal privilege which confirms all our statutes and laudable customs. As this book would alter them, or at least would prejudice the confirmatory privilege, I suggest that we do not consent to the Bishop's proposal for a further meeting if it is to meddle with them.' Precentor Burton declared himself 'an obedient son of the Church of Rome,' so he protested that he would not withdraw himself from her gracious favours. Macworth and Burton, however, would not dissociate themselves from the unanimous consent to the proposed meeting being held on 29 May, 1442, while asking that their protest should be recorded. *L.C.S.* iii. 453–456; 457.

1442. May 29. The Bishop attends for the 40th meeting of the D. and C. Dean Macworth expressly refuses to consent to this adjourned meeting and firmly refuses to consent to the new book of statutes or to new orders, as

he believed that if he did so it would redound to the prejudice of his dignity. *L.C.S.* iii. 457, 458.

1443. March 22; third Friday in Lent. Before Mr J. Derby, commissary, the dean of Christianity, represented by Rob. Stevenot, proves that Dean Macworth was named in a certain mandate (from the Bp). W. Freston appears for Macworth who (he states) is engaged as rector of Tredyngton, dio. of Worc., shriving parishioners. A mandate procuratorial is exhibited on the Dean's behalf and the matter is deferred till April 2, when T. Meburn (his proctor) gives notice of appeal, and J. Scotte, as mandatory from the court of Canterbury, inhibits the Bp's commissary from proceeding further against the Dean. *L.C.S.* iii. 458–460.

1443. April 29, '*post nonam*,' precentor, chancellor, treasurer, subdean, etc. meet in presence of the Bp to discuss the regimen of the *communa*, and the offices of provost and master of the fabric. (These are dealt with in Particula v. of *Nov. Reg.*) *L.C.S.* iii. 462, 463; cf. 354–357.

1443 May 20. Bp Alnwick receives express approval from canons, and tacit assent from Dean, to his Statute *de modo incensandi chorum.* Chancellor Partrich complains that the Dean suddenly and without due process, contrary to the intent of the *Laudum*, advised the chaplain, with whom the chancellor in compliance with *Laudum* (p. 104 above) had provided himself, [not] to wear his habit (?) in cathedral. Partrich demands an apology. *L.C.S.* iii. 464.

1444. May 1. (anno consec. 18°, et translac. 8°.) Mandate from Bp Alnwick to D. and C. to observe his statute and ordinance on the Manner and Form of Censing the Choir. *L.C.S.* iii. 509–511.

1444. Saturday, May 23. Bishop Alnwick's *Statutum de modo incensandi chorum* is received and read by the Subdean in Chapter, and accepted by them. *L.C.S.* i. 162; iii. 516 (the Statute of 1st May, as revised, Friday, May 22).

1445. Jan. 1. Rob. Burton, precentor, attacks an acolyte who was about to cense him at evensong.

1445. Jan. 2. Precentor Burton abuses an officer who came to affix the Bp's mandate in choir. *L.C.S.*

1445. Jan. 3. Commission from Bp to Dr J. Tylney, keeper of St Peter's altar and *auditor causarum.* *L.C.S.* iii. clxxxix.

1445. Bp Alnwick's visitation adjourned first to Feb. 3; then, to June 28; afterwards, to July 5. *L.C.S.* iii. 528.

1445. Feb. 6. Official of the Court of Canterbury delivers to Bp Alnwick's jurisdiction J. Scot (see 22 Mar. 1443) who had appealed from the Bishop. *L.C.S.* iii. 524, 525.

He is subsequently cited to Burden (? Buckden) church for Feb. 25th. p. 526.

1445. Feb. 6 (Saturday). Dean Makworth was excommunicated at mass in cathedral by W. Knyght, rector of (?) Estcombe, dio. Linc., in a loud voice so that his friends might hear of it, by virtue of mandate from the official of the Court of Canterbury. *L.C.S.* iii. 525.

1445. Feb. 11. Eugenius IV grants to Dean Macworth absolution from any guilt of perjury which he may have incurred from time to time by transgression of Statutes of Lincoln, which, on being received more than 30 years ago to the deanery, a major dignity with cure, he took oath to observe; with rehabilitation and decree that he cannot by reason of the aforesaid be molested in regard to his deanery or other benefices. '*Ad apostolice dignitatis.*' *C.P.L.* ix. 467, 468.

1445. March (8 and) 11. Instrument [reported to have been *forged* by T. Atkyn, notary public: see below *s. a.* 1449, Jan. 22] produced (cir. 1448–9) before Mr W. Bout, papal chaplain and *auditor causarum*, among acts of the cause between Bp Alnwick and Dean Mackworth. It alleges that in presence of Mr J. Bechamp, *Juris Utriusque Bacc.*, and Ric. Ireton, Esq., literate, of Sar. and Cov.-Lichf. dioceses, on 8 March, 1445, in the house of the Friars Preachers, Ludgate, W. Ascough (Bp of Salisbury), T. Brown (Bp of Norwich) and Mr Adam Moleyns, D.C.L. (Keeper of the Privy Seal), as arbitrators appointed by J. Stafford Abp of Canterbury, with regard to Dean J. Macworth's appeal to the apostolic See from grievances by Bp W. Alnewick and W. Byconell' official of the court of Canterbury and J. Stevenes president of the same court, and respecting the Dean having procured citation of the Bishop from Sir Malatesta de Capitaneis *auditor causarum* of the apostolic see, did persuade the Bp and the Dean to give up further litigation, and did prevail upon the Dean to abandon appeals in the Roman Court and forego the auditor's letter citing the Bishop. Further, that on March 11, in the Star chamber in Westminster palace, Dean Macworth appeared before (J. Stafford) Abp of Canterbury and J. (Kempe) Abp of York, W. (Alnewick) of Lincoln, T. (Brown) of Norwich, T. (Bourchier) of Ely, and T. (de Bekinton) of Bath and Wells, and, being pressed by them, did write a declaration that notwithstanding his appeal, against the rescript of Masters W. Byconell' and J. Stevenes of the court of Canterbury, to the Apostolic see, and notwithstanding his having procured a commission authorising Sir Malatesta de Capitaneis an *auditor causarum* of the apostolic

palace to proceed, and a citation to Bp Alnewick to appear, he now, for the sake of peace, doth renounce the said appeals, commissions, citations, &c. Finally, that the Abp of Canterbury requested Macworth (who promised so to do) with all possible haste to send letters to his counsel in the Roman court to desist from proceedings before Malatesta de Capitaneis. Bp Alnewick and Mr J. Macworth thereupon requested the notary T. Atkyn to draw up a public instrument, setting forth all the premisses, which he signed and attested with his accustomed notarial sign and signature. *C.P.L.* x. 32–34.

1446. Feb. 3. Mandate from Eugenius IV (St Peter's, Rome) to (J. Kemp) Abp of York, (T. Bekynton) Bp of Bath and the Archd. of Hainault in Liége, to publish the sentence delivered by Mr Malatesta de Capitaneis, papal chaplain and auditor, protecting Bp Alnwick from further molestation or proceedings by Dean Macworth who is condemned in costs (taxed at 20 gold florins of the *camera*) and on whom is imposed perpetual silence in the matter in dispute concerning subjection, jurisdiction, etc. (Alnwick had appealed to the Pope, being in doubt whether Macworth would obey sentence.) *C.P.L.* ix. 481.

1446. March 16. (*Entry subsequently cancelled so as to be more correctly entered below.*) The Chapter and W. Stanley, the V.C. of L., having complained to Eugenius IV that Dean J. M. has refused to give 'feedings' (*pastum*) to canons and servers, as he is bound by oath to do, on certain festivals, the Pope commissions Abp of York, (T. Bourchier) Bp of Ely, and Bp of Bath to summon the Dean and other parties and decide without appeal on all the causes which Chapter, V.C., and servers intend to bring against Macworth. '*Humilibus supplicum.*' *C.P.L.* ix. 540.

1446. July 13. Mandate from same to (J. Kempe) Abp of Y. and (T. de Bekington) Bp of Bath and Wells. The recent petition of Chapter of L. complains that certain articles, by Ric. Flemmyng then Bp of L. [27 May, 1421], had been published, but the said articles were derogatory to their statutes and customs and prejudicial to many of their own number, while it had been only a small number of canons—not all of the residentiaries even—who had been summoned to invite Bp F.'s arbitration: papal letters, said to have been issued to confirm such articles, have not hitherto been lawfully executed. Petitioners ask that Flemmyng's articles may be declared null. The mandatories are ordered to summon dean John (Macworth), hear both sides and decide without appeal. '*Humilibus supplicum.*' *C.P.L.* ix. 543.

1446. (? Sept.) Rob. Burton, Precentor, dies.

1447. Mar. 25, about 7 a.m. Bp Alnwick's commission to T. Balscote, Decr.D., J. Derby, LL.D., J. Tylney, Decr.D., J. Annsell, LL.B., J. Sutton, LL.B., to proceed canonically against J. Makworth, Dean, as is alleged ('*assertum*').

1447. Sept. 22. Ric. Dicolun (?) Dikonsun) appointed by Bp Alnwick to assist Rob. Thornton, president of the Consistory Court. *L.C.S.* iii. 532, 533.

1447. Oct. 29, Sunday. W. Stokler of Lincoln disturbs divine service in cathedral.

cir. 1447. In his long note on the topic '*Papa Romanus*' in his *Dictionarium Theologicum* (composed as Dr R. L. Poole tells us between 1434 and 1457) Dr T. Gascoigne wrote:—

"Maximum enim lucrum iam perveniens curiae papae inter cetera est hoc, quod papa vel ipsi quibus a papa causae committuntur, concedunt plura et sentenciant pro una parte, et mox instante pecunia revocant eadem prius concessa; et aliquando revocant pluries revocata, ita ut nullus sit finis conclusus in materia Romae appellata, ut nuper ostensum est in materiis controversiae episcopi Lincolniensis domini Willelmi Alnwyk, et partis sibi adversae, decani eiusdem ecclesiae, qui optavit ut totiens sibi turificaretur sicut episcopo; et, si episcopus esset praesens in ecclesia Lincoln, quod nec episcopus, nec alius, inciperet officium in ecclesia illa, quousque Decanus stallum suum intravit: ex qua controversia plurima mala secuta sunt." *Loci e libro Veritatis*, ed. Ja. E. Thorold Rogers, *Oxford*, 1881, p. 153. Cf. pp. 43, 44, 62, supra; also R. L. Poole's article 'Gascoigne, T.' in *D. Nat. Biog.*

1448. Sep. 21. Bp Alnwick delivers an award (in English) between J. Litlyngton, abbot of Croyland, and T. Lord Dacres of Holbeach. Dugdale, *Monast.* (1846) ii. 122, 123.

1449. Jan. 22. Pope Nicholas V gives a mandate to J. cardinal priest of St Balbina's, residing in England, and to T. de Bekinton Bp of Bath, to deprive T. Atkyn, notary, of his office, and otherwise punish him, and to declare void a certain public instrument (bearing date in an upper chamber in the house of Friars Preachers, by Ludgate, 8th March, and Star chamber, 11th March, 1444-5) concerning the Bp and the Dean of Lincoln, if the mandatories find that Atkyn has forged it, as J. Westgate, promoter of criminal affairs of the court of W. Alnewick Bp of Lincoln, has informed the Pope that Atkyn did. '*Si reproborum errantium.*' *C.P.L.* x. pp. 31-34.

1449. Dec. 5. W. Alnwick dies. His tomb in S.W. of

Lincoln nave. His chantry, *L. Chapter Muniments* D. ii. 50, box ii.

1450. J. Percy resigns subdeanery.

1450–51. Jan. 10. Peter Partrich (chancellor) dies.

1451. March 6. Pope Nicholas V rehabilitates J. Crosseby priest of the diocese of Carlisle, bachelor in canon and civil law, rector of Bryghtwel in Lincoln diocese, and prebendary of Thorngate and Treasurer of Lincoln (collated by Bp Alnwick, 19 Dec. 1449). Dispensation granted to hold these benefices for life, or to exchange for three compatible benefices. He had, in time gone by, committed homicide when defending himself in a quarrel with an old and turgid glover who had vexed him by not keeping his word to have a pair of new gloves ready in time for a certain occasion, and who when they were subsequently bickering drew his knife against him and received a wound. Pope Martin V had, through Marmaduke Lumley then Bp of Carlisle, previously granted Crosby dispensation to proceed to ordination and receive preferment, 8 March, 1430. (*C.P.L.* viii. 173, 443 *bis*, 601.) *Sedes apostolica, pia mater.* *C.P.L.* x. 214, 215.

1451. April 14. Further rehabilitation granted by Nicholas V to J. Crosseby, rector of Bryghtwel, who when applying for dispensation to hold the Treasurership, &c. from the present Pope had omitted to repeat the fact of his illegitimacy, as son of a priest [named], who himself had formerly been rector of the same church at Bryghtwell. '*Sedes apostolica, pia mater.*' *C.P.L.* x. 216, 217; cf. viii. 601. Treasurer Crosby survived till 26 March, 1477. He was buried in Lincoln Cathedral, and in 1531 still had a chantry at St George's altar. *L.C.S.* iii. 892.

1451. July 17. Pope Nicholas V issues a mandate to the Abp of Taranto and to T. Kempe Bp of London and T. Bourchier Bp of Ely, on the recent petition of W. Stanley vice-chancellor of Lincoln and all the ministers and *officiarii* of divine offices in the choir there (who have expressed their doubt whether J. Macworth, the Dean, will obey) to execute the definitive sentence of Mr Anthony de Thossabethis papal chaplain and auditor, wherein he decreed to be unjustifiable the Dean's refusal to feed the vice-chancellor and ministers on certain yearly feasts and other days, and the anniversaries of Kings of England and Bishops of Lincoln, whenever the Bishop is absent and the Dean present or absent, in accordance with the *Laudum* of W. Alnewick *late* Bp[1], fortified by oath of both parties, as is more

[1] See above, pp. 116, 118 (Art. 18 of Award). Cf. *L.C.S.* iii. 260, 283, 508. Also i. 73, 74; and iii. 178–180 as to the *pastus ministrorum*

fully contained in a book of the church called a Consuetudinary; the mandatories are to publish the said sentence, with another sentence issued by the same auditor in favour of the ministers and *officiarii*, where and when they think expedient, to cause the Dean to provide the feedings every year, and make satisfaction for arrears of meals, with costs; the mandatories are to aggravate the processes as often as may be expedient, invoking (if necessary) the aid of the secular arm.

The Vice-Chancellor and other petitioners had complained that their Bishop and Archbishop had denied them justice against the Dean. They mention that Nicholas V had committed their cause first to Mr Alfonsus Segura, then papal chaplain and auditor, now Bp of Mondonnedo (*Mindonien.*), and subsequently to W. de Fundera, J. Josso, and Ant. de Thossabethis. The last named had imposed perpetual silence upon Dean Macworth, condemned him, besides costs, in six gold florins of the papal *camera*, as the value of meals which he had refused to provide; also, by the second sentence, in ninety such gold florins for the feedings, and fifty for the costs taxed. '*Exhibita nobis.*' *C.P.L.* 535, 536.

1451. (Dec.) J. Mackworth dies. His tomb by S.W. pillar of (N.W. tower) 'our Lady's steeple' (S. Peck, *Desid. Curiosa*, ii. 305). Mackworth's chantry, in St George's Chapel. *Chapter Acts*, 9 July, 1457.

provided by the Canon in weekly course, according to the Consuetudinary as revised in Chapter in 1403. In *L.C.S.* vol. iii., on p. 178, insert 'quandam' before 'corruptelam' at the end of the 1st paragraph and read 'conuenit' (for 'consueuit') line 11 from bottom.

QUOMODO PSALMI A CANONICIS DICENDI SUNT.

Ab unoquoque canonico post psalmos suos dicatur

Kyrieleyson.
Christeleyson.
Kyrieleyson.

PATER noster, qui es in celis, sanctificetur nomen tuum. Adueniat regnum tuum. Fiat voluntas tua, sicut in celo et in terra. Panem nostrum quotidianum da nobis hodie. Et dimitte nobis debita nostra, sicut et nos dimittimus debitoribus nostris.

V. Et ne nos inducas in tentationem:
R. Sed libera nos a malo. Amen.
V. Saluos fac seruos et ancillas tuas:
R. Domine Deus meus, sperantes in te.
V. Anime famulorum famularumque tuarum requiescant in pace. *R.* Amen.
V. Domine, exaudi oracionem meam:
R. Et clamor meus ad te veniat.

V. Dominus vobiscum:
R. Et cum spiritu tuo.
Oremus.

OMNIPOTENS sempiterne Deus, qui vivorum dominaris simul et mortuorum, omniumque misereris quos tuos fide et opere futuros esse prenoscis: te supplices exoramus, ut pro quibus effundere preces decrevimus, quosque vel presens seculum adhuc in carne retinet vel futurum jam exutos corpore suscepit, pietatis tue clemencia omnium delictorum suorum veniam et gaudia consequi mereantur eterna; per Dominum nostrum Qui tecum vivit et regnat in unitate Spiritus Sancti Deus per omnia secula seculorum. Amen.

V. Dominus vobiscum:
R. Et cum spiritu tuo.
V. Benedicamus Domino:
R. Deo gracias.

FROM SAINT HUGH'S ORDER FOR THE CANONS' DAILY PSALTER (LINCOLN).

To be said by each Canon after his Psalms.

Lord, have mercy upon us.
Christ, have mercy upon us.
Lord, have mercy upon us.

Our Father, &c.
And lead us not into temptation.
But deliver us from evil. Amen.

O Lord, save Thy servants and handmaidens:
Who put their trust in Thee.
May the souls of Thy servants and handmaidens rest in peace. Amen.
Lord, hear my prayer:
And let my crying come unto Thee.

The Lord be with you:
And with thy spirit.
Let us pray.

ALMIGHTY Everlasting God, who art Lord both of the living and of the dead, and pitiest all those whom Thou dost foreknow to be Thine by faith and works: we humbly beseech Thee that those for whom we have determined to offer our prayers, both those whom this world yet holdeth in the flesh, and those already unclothed of the body, whom the world to come hath received, may by Thy goodness and mercy be counted worthy to attain pardon of all their sins, and eternal joys, through our Lord and Saviour Jesus Christ, Who liveth and reigneth with Thee and the Holy Ghost, One God, world without end. Amen.

The Lord be with you.
And with thy spirit.
Bless we the Lord.
Thanks be to God.

INDEX

For EU product safety concerns, contact us at Calle de José Abascal, 56–1°, 28003 Madrid, Spain or eugpsr@cambridge.org.

www.ingramcontent.com/pod-product-compliance
Ingram Content Group UK Ltd.
Pitfield, Milton Keynes, MK11 3LW, UK
UKHW012335130625
459647UK00009B/305

* 9 7 8 1 1 0 7 4 4 8 1 7 9 *